nīhithaw ācimowina

ᓂᐦᐃᖬᐤ ᐋᒋᒧᐃᐧᓇ

Woods Cree Stories

FIRST NATIONS LANGUAGE READERS

WOODS CREE

nīhithaw ācimowina

ᓀᐦᐃᖬᐤ ᐋᒋᒧᐃᐧᓇ

Woods Cree Stories

Written and translated by
Solomon Ratt

Illustrated by Holly Martin

FIRST NATIONS UNIVERSITY OF CANADA

University of Regina Press

Printed and bound in Canada at GoLibro. The text of this book is printed on 100% post-consumer recycled paper with earth-friendly vegetable-based inks.

COVER AND TEXT DESIGN: Duncan Campbell, University of Regina Press.

EDITOR FOR THE PRESS: Donna Grant, University of Regina Press.

The artwork in this volume is by Holly Martin, a Swampy Cree artist originally from Moose Lake First Nation.

LIBRARY AND ARCHIVES CANADA CATALOGUING IN PUBLICATION
Cataloguing in Publication (CIP) data available at the Library and Archives Canada web site: *www.collectionscanada.gc.ca* and at *www.uofrpress.ca/publications/Woods-Cree-Stories*

U OF R PRESS

University of Regina Press, University of Regina
Regina, Saskatchewan, Canada, S4S 0A2
TEL: (306) 585-4758 FAX: (306) 585-4699
WEB: www.uofrpress.ca

The University of Regina Press acknowledges the support of the Creative Industry Growth and Sustainability program, made possible through funding provided to the Saskatchewan Arts Board by the Government of Saskatchewan through the Ministry of Parks, Culture, and Sport. We acknowledge the financial support of the Government of Canada through the Canada Book Fund for our publishing activities. We acknowledge the support of the Canada Council for the Arts for our publishing program.

Saskatchewan Arts Board

Canadian Heritage Patrimoine canadien

Government of Saskatchewan

University of Regina

Canada Council for the Arts Conseil des Arts du Canada

MIX
Paper from responsible sources
FSC® C100212

CONTENTS

Foreword

This is the fourth volume in the First Nations Language Readers series, and the first follow-up to the Cree volume, *wawiyatācimowinisa / Funny Little Stories,* that introduced the series. As indicated at the time, the first volume was a mixture of dialects and genres, sampling the possibilities of themes that individual volumes in this series might explore. In the present texts, we are fortunate to be able to highlight the storytelling and dialect of Solomon Ratt, a Woods Cree speaker and educator from *āmaciwīspimowinihk* (Stanley Mission, Saskatchewan). The stories in this collection are the product of course preparation for the classes Solomon has developed over the years at the First Nations University of Canada (formerly the Saskatchewan Indian Federated College), and all are infused with his particular sense of humour. Humour is not only the best medicine; it is also an exceptionally useful teaching tool.

Fortunately, these stories can now flow beyond the classroom and find new life in the larger audience of readers who will be able to enjoy them. Make no mistake—all remain welcome to join Solomon in his classes at FNUniv where many more stories and his signature brand of humour await.

The common theme here is the Cree language—teaching it, sharing it, keeping it alive and giving it a chance to flourish. We hope this will serve as one more contribution in the ongoing efforts to reverse the trend of language loss suffered by so many in the Indigenous language communities of the world. That is one goal of the First Nations Language Readers series. That is the goal of the Language and Linguistics programs at First Nations University and all of our partners throughout the world who understand the value inherent in each and every human language.

ahkami-nīhithawīk ikwa mōcikihtāk!

Arok Wolvengrey
pāskāwihowi-pīsim, 2014

Introduction

These stories are a result of years of teaching the Cree language at First Nations University. I have often found a lack of relevant materials to accompany my class topics so I end up writing stories to highlight some aspect of Cree culture or Cree grammar. A thank you to all my former students who have been patient with me and laughed at my weird sense of humour. A special thank you to my friend and colleague Arok Wolvengrey, who is most instrumental in getting this collection of stories off the ground (in jest, I call him "slave-driver"). Had I been left to my own devices I would have left these in my files only to revive them when I needed them for class.

Some of these stories have appeared elsewhere. Four stories—"Boys Get Lost," "Long Ago Christmas," "Grandmother's Bay," and "Shaking Spear and the Bear"— appear in *A Woods Cree Grammar and Workbook* in a slightly different form (Ratt, 2009). I have used "Shaking-Spear Wanders About" in various editions in the course packs for Cree 101, which I have used for many years.

A special "thank you" to my former student Holly Martin for the artwork. I remember when I introduced "Buffalo

Wings" in class and I saw her doodle while I was reading the story to the class. After the class she stopped by and handed me a picture of a buffalo with wings. Holly originally comes from Moose Lake, but currently lives in Thompson, Manitoba. I'm grateful that she agreed to share her artistic gifts to further enliven these stories.

Whereas many of these stories are my own, I have also included the traditional story of "Wīsahkīcāhk and the Startlers" as the first entry in this collection. Cree stories have been the main teaching tool in traditional Cree society. When I teach this story, I not only try to use the traditional mode, but I also include the following piece on the role of Cree stories and the lessons behind the stories. Before reading on, you may wish to read the story of "Wīsahkīcāhk and the Startlers," either in syllabics on pages 3–5, or in the Standard Roman Orthography for Cree with English translation on pages 39–45.

Language and Culture: What Do Our Stories Tell Us?

Language and culture are interdependent. Without a common language there would be no culture. Culture is learned during the course of a person's life. More important, however, is the idea that culture is acquired while growing up. Acquiring a culture is mostly an unconscious activity while learning involves conscious effort. No amount of formal training can help in the acquisition of culture. I learned the English language but I still find myself out of my element in "polite" society—I have been in a state of culture shock for most of my life! Yet, a child growing up acquires both language and culture with few problems, needing formal schooling only for the technical skills of reading and writing at a later date to complete their education.

In oral traditions, such as those of the Native Americans,

culture was passed on through the use of language in ceremonies, daily activities, and stories. The stories were told each winter and in each subsequent winter the process of enculturation went a step further, with the process continuing to adulthood. Without a break in this process and without the aid of "formal" schooling came the acquisition of language and culture. Having grown to adulthood partaking in the ceremonies, daily life, and stories, a person had a well-rounded education: childrearing, spousal responsibility, respect, patience, kindliness, tolerance, and love—all were covered in this education. What would happen, however, if this process of enculturation were to be interrupted, intruded upon, by a foreign language, a foreign culture?

My education was interrupted by my schooling—at the age of six, going-on-seven in three months' time, I was taken from my parents to go to a residential school. I still speak my language—but that's because my generation was lucky in that we were not punished for using our language at the residential school like so many before us. I still speak my language—but that's because my late parents spoke nothing but Cree when we were home for two months in the summer. I still speak my language—but because I was home only during the summer I missed out on the stories told in the winter and thus I found myself lacking in my cultural knowledge. But hey! My elders told me to "learn the cunning of the Whiteman"—that phrase is a direct quote from Alexander Morris during the negotiations for Treaty Four. So I learned the "cunning of the Whiteman": I learned to read—first English, then Cree—and I learned to love the search for knowledge. I came across many Cree narratives—most in English, but some in both Cree and English—and I began my own enculturation to go beyond the level of a six-turning-seven-year-old child—beyond that point when my education got interrupted by my schooling.

I found that my schooling became part of my education!

Let us consider the story of those poor Startlers. What is this story about? At first glance, it seems to be just an amusing scatological story. Sadly enough, that is as far as most people get with the story of "Wīsahkīcāhk and the Startlers." When we get beyond the surface, however, we can see that the story contains some key elements about Cree culture. The story of "Wīsahkīcāhk and the Startlers" contains lessons about the sanctity of names, about respect, honour, patience, communal consultation, and communal action against a common enemy.

Teaching through Wīsahkīcāhk's actions usually involves symbolic inversions. In this case, Wīsahkīcāhk addresses the Startlers in a common way that shows respect to the ones he addresses and that his intentions are honourable. The *-itik* at the end of *nisīmitik* is known as an honorific, a signal that Wīsahkīcāhk is supposed to be respectful and honourable. That his *actions* toward the Startlers are less than honourable and that he shows utter contempt to them is a symbolic inversion that highlights the virtues of honour and respect. In short, we learn by Wīsahkīcāhk's negative example of how to behave. Everyone is deserving of honour and respect no matter how small!

Another lesson conveyed in the story of Wīsahkīcāhk and the Startlers is about the sanctity of names. In the days when we all had Cree names we knew those names were sacred and we used them sparingly. We addressed people by how we were related to them, not by their names. Telling the story of the Startlers questions the validity of the sanctity of names. Wīsahkīcāhk shows utter contempt to the Startlers by defecating on them; this suggests that we must still be on guard about our names, lest someone abuses us like the Startlers were abused. The danger of revealing one's name to someone outside of the family, especially a high-sounding name like *okoskohowīsak,* opens one to ridicule because, upon reflection, the name *okoskohowīsak* sounds like a boast about one's character.

Two other lessons appear in the story of the Startlers. These lessons deal with community involvement and having the patience to see a project through. People in a community need to consult with each other much like the Startlers do about Wīsahkīcāhk's actions. The Startlers agreed to get their revenge on Wīsahkīcāhk and acted in unison. Most of the Startlers waited in the bushes as Wīsahkīcāhk tried four times to jump across the river. The first three times a few of the younger grouse flew up, but on his fourth attempt they all flew up to startle him. It is understandable that a few of the younger birds would rush ahead, but all in all the lesson comes across that being patient to achieve a common goal is worth the wait.

The loss of our oral tradition leads to the loss of our language and the loss of our language leads to the loss of our culture. Without our stories we lose those lessons about respect, honour, child-rearing, spousal responsibility—everything needed to lead a well-adjusted and happy life. Stories like "Wīsahkīcāhk and the Startlers" are no longer told in the family unit. In the past, these stories tightened the bonds of family. Without our stories, we lose that family closeness which the telling of these stories promoted. We need to tell these stories to our young. While it seems no longer feasible to acquire the lessons through a close family gathering every winter, we must make a conscious effort to have our children learn these lessons through formal lessons in the classroom.

Solomon Ratt

Notes on the Text

These stories are written in the Woods Cree dialect of Solomon Ratt's home community of Stanley Mission (*āmaciwīspimowinihk*), Saskatchewan. This means that they are presented in a 'th' dialect, which can be compared with the 'y' (or Plains) and 'n' (or Swampy) dialects. As illustrated in Table 1, there are two main features that are usually used to distinguish Woods Cree from other Cree dialects.

The most important feature is the occurrence of the 'th' (or [ð]) sound, similar to the sound at the beginning of English ***th****is* or ***th****at* (but not the same as at the beginning of ***th****in* or the end of *wi****th***). This sound occurs only in Woods Cree and wherever it occurs, it will generally alternate with a 'y' sound in Plains Cree, and an 'n' sound in Swampy Cree (see the word for 'I; me' in Table 1). The second feature involves the occurrence of the two long vowels, /ī/ (similar to the sound in English *b****ea****t*) and /ē/ (similar to the sound in English *b****ai****t*). Most Cree dialects use both of these vowels, but both Woods and northern Plains Cree dialects pronounce both as /ī/ (see the word for "go home").

The final example in Table 1 also illustrates another feature of Solomon's dialect, the shortening of vowels before combinations of /h/ and another consonant (hC or the so-called 'pre-aspirated consonants'). Thus, what appears as /pēht-/ in southern Plains and Swampy Cree, and /pīht-/ in northern Plains, sounds closer to [piht-] in Woods Cree. This loss of vowel length before pre-aspirated consonants is not exclusive to Solomon's dialect or Woods Cree in general, but such vowels are still often written as long. In contrast, these vowels are generally written short before pre-aspirated consonants in these texts. This is similar to the alternation of /ī/ and /i/ before /y/ in Plains Cree. Although it always sounds long before /y/, it is generally written short (cf. Plains *niya* 'I; me' with Woods *nītha*; Plains *miyo-* 'good' with Woods *mitho-*; or Woods Cree *piyak* 'one' with Plains *pēyak*). There are other instances of /ī/ (or /ē/) being shortened in Woods Cree as well—as in ***i****yako* 'that' (cf. *ēwako*), ***i****kwa* 'and, then' (cf. *ēkwa*), and ***i****kotī* 'over there' (cf. *ēkotē*).

A couple of additional features of Solomon's dialect can be mentioned here. One involves the "light" and "heavy" reduplicative preverbs (cf. Ahenakew and Wolfart 1983).

	th ~ y ~ n	ī / ē	VhC
Dialect	'I; me'	'go home'	'I hear it'
Woods	nī**th**a	kīw**ī**	nip**i**htīn
northern Plains	ni**y**a	kīw**ī**	nip**ī**htīn
southern Plains	ni**y**a	kīw**ē**	nip**ē**htēn
Swampy	nī**n**a	kīw**ē**	nip**ē**htēn

Table 1. Western Cree Dialect Features

The use of *ay-* is common in Western dialects when accompanying a vowel-initial verb stem (e.g., *ati-**ay**-āmaciwīw* 'he began climbing up the hill'), and it indicates an ongoing or continuous action. Where so-called "heavy reduplication" occurs to indicate intermittent or repetitive actions, it is often represented as *āh-* before vowel-initial stems. In Solomon's dialect, however, this preverb is consistently represented as *āy-* (e.g., *ī-**āy**-asotamākīcik* 'as they kept making promises'). The alternation of /y/ and /h/ (and even /w/) as glides is quite common across western dialects, but the precise pattern differs community to community.

Another dialect feature involving the glide /w/ is its effect on preceding short vowels /a/ and /i/. When the sequences /aw/ and /iw/ occur, they most frequently sound more like [ow]. Sometimes, the original /aw/ or /iw/ sequence can be recovered from dialect-internal evidence (e.g. *miyāsk**aw*** [miya:skow] will become *ī-miyāsk**ā**kot* [not *ī-miyāsk**ō**kot]). However, some instances never occur in a position to show such alternation, and so the <ow> spelling has been adopted, as in *powāt-* 'dream about someone' (cf. Plains *pawāt-*).

In general, these dialect features are noted here to explain differences in the Standard Roman Orthography spellings. This will also affect the use of syllabics and the glossary listings of words and thus be important for each of the major sections of the current volume.

Woods Cree Syllabics

In the first section, **ᓀᐦᐃᖬᐤ ᐋᒋᒧᐏᓇ**, all texts are given in Woods Cree syllabics (see Figure 1 on page xviii). This differs only slightly from the Western Cree Syllabary (cf. Wolvengrey 2007) due to the aforementioned sound changes required for Woods Cree. The major feature specific to

Woods Cree is simply the inclusion of a series of symbols for the 'th' (or [ð]) sound (e.g. ᖬ = tha) which does not occur in any other dialect. This series resembles the /y/ symbol (e.g. ᔭ = ya), which is the sound that typically alternates with 'th' in the 'y'-dialect, Plains Cree. This feature is fairly easy for other dialect readers to adapt to. Wherever a 'th' symbol occurs, a Plains Cree reader can read it as the same as the corresponding 'y', while a Swampy Cree reader can treat it as the same as the corresponding 'n' series (e.g. ᓇ = na) – with one additional complication.

Because Woods Cree has only six vowels, the syllabic symbols usually used for the /ē/ vowels (e.g. ᐁ = Plains Cree /ē/; ᐯ = /pē/, etc.) in most other syllabic systems are instead used for Woods Cree /ī/ sounds (e.g. ᐁ = Woods Cree /ī/; ᐯ = /pī/, etc.). In turn, this means that symbols representing the short vowel /i/ (ᐃ, ᐱ, etc.) are never marked as long in Woods Cree syllabics as they are in Plains Cree (ᐄ, ᐲ, etc.). Thus, the overposed dot is only needed to mark two vowels as long: /ō/ (ᐆ, ᐴ, etc.) and /ā/ (ᐋ, ᐹ, etc.).

In practical terms, the Woods Cree Syllabary is sufficient to represent the Woods Cree dialect, and readers of other dialects need only remember that the /ē/ series is to be read as /ī/ for Woods Cree. This may take some getting used to, as the symbols used for this sound will match /ē/ for Plains and Swampy Cree, leading to the appearance of an over-abundance of /ē/ syllables. Sometimes this correspondence works well.

For instance, the symbol ᐯ can be read as *pē-* in Swampy and southern Plains Cree and as *pī-* in Woods and northern Plains Cree, each meaning 'come towards' as appropriate in each dialect. Similarly, the spelling ᒣᑕᐍ will correspond with southern Plains and Swampy *mētawē* and northern Plains and Woods Cree *mītawī*, both meaning 'play'. How-

	ī	i	o	a	ō	ā	finals
	ᐁ	ᐃ	ᐅ	ᐊ	ᐆ	ᐋ	
w	ᐍ	ᐏ	ᐓ	ᐘ	ᐕ	ᐚ	ᐤ
p	ᐯ	ᐱ	ᐳ	ᐸ	ᐴ	ᐹ	ᑊ
t	ᑌ	ᑎ	ᑐ	ᑕ	ᑑ	ᑖ	ᐟ
k	ᑫ	ᑭ	ᑯ	ᑲ	ᑰ	ᑳ	ᐠ
c	ᒉ	ᒋ	ᒍ	ᒐ	ᒎ	ᒑ	ᐨ
m	ᒣ	ᒥ	ᒧ	ᒪ	ᒨ	ᒫ	ᒼ
n	ᓀ	ᓂ	ᓄ	ᓇ	ᓅ	ᓈ	ᐣ
s	ᓭ	ᓯ	ᓱ	ᓴ	ᓲ	ᓵ	ᐢ
y	ᔦ	ᔨ	ᔪ	ᔭ	ᔫ	ᔮ	ᐩ
th	ᖧ	ᖨ	ᖪ	ᖬ	ᖫ	ᖭ	‡

l ᓬ	r ᕒ	h ᐦ	hk ᕽ

Figure 1. Woods Cree Syllabary

ever, in other cases, a Woods (or northern Plains) Cree word will not convert to the appropriate southern Plains or Swampy form. For instance, the Woods Cree spelling ᓭᐯˣ (*sīpīhk* 'at the river'), would seem to correspond with southern Plains and Swampy 'sēpēhk', when in fact the appropriate form for all dialects is *sīpīhk*. Therefore, it is important to know which dialect, and thus which version of the Syllabary, is being represented in any given text. As already mentioned, this collection uses the Woods Cree Syllabary exclusively.

Note must also be made of the form of punctuation used in the syllabic section. Traditionally, little to no punctuation was used in Cree syllabic texts. In writing, and even in some printing, words were simply broken at the end of a line whenever the writer or typesetter ran out of space. Word breaks were otherwise uncommon and fairly long verbal constructions, including a number of preverbs, might all be written without any break at all, as in the second and third words in (1).

(1) ᐱᓭᑳᐧᐤ ᐁᑫᒫᑎᓈᐃᐧᑫᓯᑳᐠ ᓂᑫᓅᐦᑌᐃᐢᐸᖭᐣ

No other punctuation, with the possible marking of sentence breaks (with a period or lowered x final), was common.

In the current volume, however, some limited punctuation and word break conventions have been introduced. Although periods are the only punctuation marks used, varying lengths of spaces help replace some other conventions of the Standard Roman Orthography (SRO). A single space is used to indicate a word internal boundary that is represented by a hyphen in the SRO. Thus, the words in (1) above will actually be represented as in (2) (with SRO equivalent provided).

(2) ᐱᔭᑳᐧᐤ   ᐁ ᑭ ᒫᑎᓈᐃᐧ ᑭᓯᑳᐠ   ᓂᑭ ᓄᐦᑎ ᐃᐢᐸᖬᐣ
[piyakwāw ī-kī-mātināwi-kīsikāk nikī-nohtī-ispathin ...]

In contrast, full words are separated by two spaces, as also illustrated in (2). Even larger breaks of three spaces are used to indicate the equivalent of phrases, clauses or sentences which are offset by commas, semi-colons, colons, periods, and exclamation, question and/or quotations marks in the roman orthography. This compromise obviously does not add a great deal of punctuation to the traditional representation of syllabics, but will hopefully somewhat ease the process of reading for those who are trying to learn.

Finally, English words found in the Cree texts are simply presented in the regular English spelling (in italics), and no attempt has been made to translate or otherwise present the words in either Cree orthography. This convention thus applies to both the syllabics and to the SRO.

Woods Cree SRO and English Translation

In the second section of this volume, the stories are given in both the Cree Standard Roman Orthography (SRO) and English translation on facing pages for ease of reference for language learners. This has been standard practice in recent Algonquian text publications (e.g., Ahenakew 1986, 1987b; Bear et al. 1998; Beardy 1988; Ellis 1995, Kā-Nīpitēhtēw 1998, Minde 1997) and in the preceding volumes of this First Nations Language Reader series (Wolvengrey 2007, Cote 2011). The conventions of the Cree SRO, as described by Wolfart and Ahenakew (1987) and Okimāsis and Wolvengrey (2008), are followed, with the modifications required by Woods Cree. Thus, no /ē/ vowel is necessary, and the [ð] sound of the Woods dialect is indicated by the digraph 'th', following the conventional use of the Gift of Language and Culture and the Lac La Ronge Indian Band Curriculum Unit (cf. Ratt 2009). In marking long vowels, the macron (or overposed hyphen) is used (i.e., ā, ī, ō) in preference to the circumflex (i.e., â, î, ô). Both of these means of marking the long Cree vowels are in common use and, now that macrons are more readily available in computer fonts, we continue the more recent practice of using macrons (cf. Okimāsis 2004; Ratt 2009; Wolvengrey 2001, 2007).

Preceding each story will be a title page, accompanied by a wonderful piece of artwork depicting a scene from the story itself. We are grateful to Holly Martin, a young Swampy Cree artist originally from Moose Lake, Manitoba, for adding these visual elements to the images conjured by Solomon's words.

Woods Cree-English Glossary

The final section of this volume is a Woods Cree-to-English glossary or word list containing all the nouns, verbs, particles, preverbs, etc., found within the Cree texts, with accompanying word class and translation. The form of this glossary closely follows the standards established by Wolfart and Ahenakew (1987; cf. also Ahenakew 1986, 1987b; Beardy 1988; Kā-Nīpitēhtēw 1998; Minde 1997, etc.) as modified by Wolvengrey (2007) in the first Cree volume in this series. As such, the glossary includes Cree entries listed in their base or stem form (as indicated with verbs, nouns, preverbs and prenouns by a following hyphen; e.g., *wāpam-* VTA; *pōni-* IPV), and these stems may or may not match the actual spoken form of a full word recognized by a fluent speaker. To a certain extent, then, it is unavoidable with this type of glossary that some knowledge of the structure of Cree words is required to find the parts of words isolated in the entries. However, the current glossary at least has the added feature of including actual textual examples of the full words along with the stem form entries. For example, the word *kā-ati-nohtīkatīt* is found in text 9, but it is the constituent parts of this word that will be found in the glossary, listed separately under *kā-* IPV, *ati-* IPV, and *nohtīkatī-* VAI. However, all three of these separate references could include as an example of their use, the full word as found in the text (i.e., *kā-ati-nohtīkatīt* 'when s/he begins to get hungry').

Most entries will have examples of this type included. However, this is not done with particles (IPC), which only occur in isolation in a single form. Similarly, many nouns occur only in their singular forms, which are usually the same as the stem forms. Only in cases when a noun occurs in a form other than the singular (i.e., plural, locative, etc.) are textual examples included with the stem entry. For those wishing for more information on stem forms, please consult appropriate grammatical or structural descriptions of Cree such as those found in Ahenakew (1987a), Okimāsis (2004), Ratt (2009), Wolfart (1973), Wolfart and Ahenakew (1987), and Wolvengrey (2001).

Another feature of this volume's glossary is in its treatment of "dependent" or "bound" noun stems. These are noun stems which cannot occur without some person-marking prefix, and they are listed in two places in the glossary. Again, following the glossaries of Ahenakew and Wolfart, all bound stems are given in bare stem form (with preceding hyphen) at the beginning of the glossary. However, since not all readers will be familiar with the analysis of bound stems into their constituent parts minus person indicators, such stems are also listed in the appropriate section of the alphabetized glossary, depending on the form they take in the text. If a bound noun stem is marked with a first person prefix (e.g., */n-/*, */ni-/* or */nit-/*), it will appear in the bound stem section and in the "n" section. For instance, a word like *nikāwīnān*, found in text 2, will be listed twice in the glossary: first, in the form of the bound, unmarked stem *-kāwiy-* 'mother', and second, under the person-marked form *nikāwīnān* 'our mother'. Similarly, if a bound noun stem is marked with a second person prefix (e.g., */k-/*, */ki-/* or */kit-/*), it will appear in the bound stem section and the "k" section. If it is marked with one of the third person prefixes, (i.e., */o-/*, */ot-/* or */w-/*), it will be found in the bound stem section and the "o" or "w" section as appropriate. On rare occasions, a bound stem is cited in the unspecfied possessor form (i.e., with prefix */m-/* or */mi-/*), and in such cases, the stem is found in both the bound stem and "m" sections. This double-listing allows easier access to bound stems in the glossary for all readers, regardless of the level of their training in Cree language structure. A similar feature is utilized by Wolvengrey (2001) in *nēhiýawēwin: itwēwina / Cree: Words*, where all bound stems are given in volume 1 (Cree-English) in the appropriate person-marked forms ("m", "n", "o" or "w" sections), but provided as unmarked stem forms in translation of English terms in volume 2 (English-Cree).

One final feature of the glossary in this volume has to do merely with a refinement in the classification of the major word classes: noun, verb, and particle. Nouns, of course, continue to be classified as animate (NA) and inanimate (NI), but are also grouped into one of four morphological subclasses based on stem type. Regular nouns are class 1 (i.e., NA_1 and NI_1), nouns that end in a sequence of vowel-glide are class 2 (i.e., NA_2 and NI_2), nouns that end in a "hidden" /w/ are class 3 (i.e., NA_3 and NI_3), while the most restricted class of single-syllable stems are class 4 (i.e., NA_4 and NI_4) (cf. Wolvengrey forthcoming). A very similar classification is made for the four subclasses of transitive animate verbs (e.g., VTA_1, VTA_2, etc.; cf. Okimāsis 2004). Transitive inanimate stems (VTI) are subdivided into three classes: class 1 (VTI_1), ending in the imperative theme vowel /a/; class 2 (VTI_2), ending in the theme vowel /ā/; and class 3 (VTI_3), as a very restricted and irregular class (e.g., *mīci-*). The intransitive verb classes are simply divided into stems that end in vowels (VAI_1 and VII_1) versus those that end in a stem-final /n/ (VAI_2 and VII_2). Each of these subclasses has morphological consequences for inflected verb forms.

The heterogeneous class of particles has received relatively little attention, generally all grouped together as IPC (indeclinable particles). The current glossary takes a first step in differentiating two important functional subclasses, recognizing temporal (IPT) and locative (IPL) particles, which indicate time and place respectively. It is expected that further refinements will be made to the classification of Cree particles in future work. In the meantime, it is hoped that the current glossary will aid both those attempting to learn the Woods Cree language and those who already speak the language but wish to delve further into literacy and the wonderful structure of *nīhithawīwin* (Woods Cree).

Arok Wolvengrey

References

Ahenakew, Freda. 1987a. *Cree Language Structures: A Cree Approach*. Winnipeg: Pemmican Publications Inc.

Ahenakew, Freda, ed. 1986. *kiskinwahamawākan-ācimowinisa / Student Stories*. Algonquian and Iroquoian Linguistics, Memoir 2. Winnipeg: Algonquian and Iroquoian Linguistics.

———. 1987b. *wāskahikaniwiyiniw-ācimowina / Stories of the House People*. Publications of the Algonquian Text Society. Winnipeg: University of Manitoba Press.

Ahenakew, Freda and H.C. Wolfart. 1983. "Productive reduplication in Plains

Cree." 369–377 in William Cowan, réd., *Actes du Quatorzième Congrès des Algonquinistes*. Ottawa: Carleton University.

Bear, Glecia, et al. 1998. *kōhkominawak otācimowiniwāwa / Our Grandmothers' Lives as Told in Their Own Words*. Edited and translated by Freda Ahenakew and H.C. Wolfart. Regina: Canadian Plains Research Center.

Beardy, L. 1988. *pisiskiwak kā-pīkiskwēcik / Talking Animals*. Edited by H.C. Wolfart. Algonquian and Iroquoian Linguistics, Memoir 5. Winnipeg: Algonquian and Iroquoian Linguistics.

Cote, Margaret, ed. 2011. *Nēnapohš āhtahsōkēwinan / Nēnapohš Legends*. First Nations Language Readers, Memoir 2. Regina: Canadian Plains Research Center.

Ellis, C. Douglas, ed. 1995. *ātalōhkāna nēsta tipācimowina / Cree Legends and Narratives from the West Coast of James Bay*. Publications of the Algonquian Text Society. Winnipeg: The University of Manitoba Press.

Kā-Nīpitēhtēw, Jim. 1998. *ana kā-pimwēwēhahk okakēskihkēmowina / The Counselling Speeches of Jim Kā-Nīpitēhtēw*. Edited and translated by Freda Ahenakew and H.C. Wolfart. Publications of the Algonquian Text Society. Winnipeg: The University of Manitoba Press.

Minde, Emma. 1997. *kwayask ē-kī-pē-kiskinowāpahtihicik / Their Example Showed Me the Way*. Edited and translated by Freda Ahenakew and H.C. Wolfart. Edmonton: The University of Alberta Press.

Okimāsis, Jean. 2004. *Cree, Language of the Plains*. 2nd, revised edition. Regina: Canadian Plains Research Center.

Okimāsis, Jean, and Arok Wolvengrey. 2008. *How to Spell it in Cree*. Regina: *miywāsin* ink.

Ratt, Solomon. 2009. *A Woods Cree Grammar and Workbook*, revised edition. Gift of Language and Culture. La Ronge, SK: Lac La Ronge Indian Band Curriculum Resource Unit.

Wolfart, H.C. 1973. *Plains Cree: A Grammatical Study*. American Philosophical Society Transactions, n.s. 63, pt. 5. Philadelphia.

Wolfart, H.C., and Freda Ahenakew. 1987. "Notes on the Orthography and the Glossary." 113–125 in Freda Ahenakew, ed., *wāskahikaniwiyiniw-ācimowina / Stories of the House People*. Winnipeg: The University of Manitoba Press.

Wolvengrey, Arok. 2001. *nēhiýawēwin: itwēwina / Cree: Words*. Volumes 1 & 2. Regina: Canadian Plains Research Center.

———. forthcoming. *Plains Cree Nouns: Inflection*. Regina: *miywāsin* ink.

Wolvengrey, Arok, ed. 2007. *wawiyatācimowinisa / Funny Little Stories*. First Nations Language Readers, Memoir 1. Regina: Canadian Plains Research Center.

ᑯᐦᐃᔭᐤ ᐋᒋᒧᐃᐧᑭ

(1) ᐁᐧᓴᐦᑫᒑᕽ ᐃᑲᐧ ᐅᑯᐢᑯᐦᐅᐁᐧᓴᐠ

ᐱᔭᑳᐧᐤ ᐁᓴ ᐁᐧᓴᐦᑫᒑᕽ ᑫ ᐸ ᐱᒧᐦᑌᐤ. ᑫᑕᐦᑕᐁᐧ ᐁᓴ ᐋᐧᐸᒣᐤ ᐱᖧᓯᓴ.

ᐦᐅ. ᓂᓭᒥᑎᐠ. ᐃᑌᐤ ᐁᓴ. ᑲᓇᐚᐸᒥᑯᐤ ᐆᐦᐅ ᐱᖧᓯᓴ. ᓂᓭᒥᑎᐠ ᐱᖧᓯᓴᐠ ᑖᓂᓯ ᑳ ᐃᑎᑲᐃᐧᔦᐠ.

ᓵᓴᐩ ᑭᐃᐧᐦᖬᓈᐣ ᐱᖧᓯᓴᐠ ᑳ ᐃᑌᐧᔭᐣ ᐃᑯᓯ ᑳ ᐃᑎᑲᐃᐧᔮᕽ.

ᓇᒪ. ᑲᐦᑭᖬᐤ ᐊᐃᐧᔭᐠ ᐊᐊᐧᓯᒣᐢ ᐃᐧᐦᖭᐤ. ᑖᐱᐢᑰᐨ ᓀᖬ ᐁᐧᓴᐦᑫᒑᕽ ᓂᑎᓯᖬᐦᑳᓱᐣ ᒫᑲ ᐅᐢᑌᓯᒫᐤ ᒦᓇ ᓂᑎᑎᑲᐃᐧᐣ. ᐦᐊᐤ ᑖᓂᓯ ᑫᖬᐚᐤ ᑳ ᐃᑎᑲᐃᐧᔦᐠ

ᓇᒨᖬ ᓂᑲ ᑫ ᐃᐧᐦᑌᓈᐣ. ᓂᓀᑭᐦᐃᑯᓈᓇᐠ ᐆᑯ ᓂᑫ ᐃᐧᐦᑕᒫᑯᓈᓇᐠ ᐁᑳ ᑕ ᐃᐧᐦᑕᒫᕽ ᑯᑕᐠ ᓂᐃᐧᐦᖪᐃᐧᓂᓈᐣ ᐅᑯᐢᑯᐦᐅᐁᐧᓴᐠ ᐁ ᐃᑎᑲᐃᐧᔮᕽ.

ᐅᑯᐢᑯᐦᐅᐁᐧᓴᐠ. ᐦᐊ. ᑳ ᐃᓯ ᐸᐦᐱᐦᐋᐟ ᐁᓴ. ᐁᓴᐩ ᐅᑯᐢᑯᐦᐅᐁᐧᓴᐠ. ᓂᑕᑭᓯᐩ ᐅᑯᐢᑯᐦᐅᐁᐧᓴᐠ ᐃᑌᐧᐤ ᐁᓴ ᐁ ᐊᑎ ᒣ̇ᓴᑖᐟ ᐃᑲᐧ ᐊᓂᐦᐃ ᑳ ᐸᑕᐦᐚᐟ ᐅᑎᓀᐤ ᐁ ᐊᑎ ᑭᒥᓴᐦᐚᑫᐟ.

ᐅᑯᐢᑯᐦᐅᐁᐧᓴᐠ. ᐅᓵᒼ ᑭᑕᐱᓭᔨᓯᓈᐚᐤ ᑕ ᑯᐢᑯᐦᐅᐁᐧᔦᐠ ᐃᑌᐤ ᐁ ᐊᑎ ᓯᐯᐧᐦᑌᐟ.

ᐅᓀᑭᐦᐃᑯᒫᐊᐧᐠ ᑯᐢᑳᐧᐱᓯᓇᐧᐠ ᐃᐢᐯ ᑳ ᐯ ᑫᐁᐧᒋᐠ.

ᐊᐁᐧᓇ ᐊᐊᐧ ᑳ ᐃᑑᑕᕽ. ᐊᐧᐦᐋᐧ. ᑲᐧᔮᐢᐠ
ᑭᐃᐧᐦᒉᑭᓯᓈᐋᐧᐤ. ᐁᓴᐩ ᐃᑌᐧᐊᐧᐠ ᐁᓴ.

ᐁᐧᓴᐦᑫᒫᕽ ᐊᓇ ᑳ ᐃᓯ ᒫᑐᐟ ᐁᓴ ᐱᔭᐠ
ᐱᖧᓯᐢ. ᐁ ᐸᐦᑲᒋᒥᑯᔮᕽ ᑕ ᐃᐧᐦᑕᒫᕽ ᑯᑕᐠ
ᑭᐃᐧᐦᖪᐃᐧᓂᓇᐤ. ᒪᔭᐤ ᐅᑯᐢᑯᐦᐅᐁᐧᓴᐠ ᐁ ᐃᑖᔮᕽ
ᑳ ᒉᓵᑎᑯᔮᕽ.

ᐦᐊᐤ ᒉᐢᑲᐧ ᐁᐧᓴᐦᑫᒫᕽ ᐃᑌᐧᐤ ᐊᐊᐧ ᓅᓴ ᐱᖧᐤ.
ᓂᑐᒉᐤ ᐁᓴ ᑲᐦᑭᖬᐤ ᐅᑑᑌᒪ ᑕ ᒫᒪᐊᐧᐱᒥᐠ.
ᑫ ᓂᑕᐃᐧ ᐯᐦᐅᐊᐧᐠ ᐱᖧᐊᐧᐠ ᐋᐧᓴᑳᐨ ᓴᐯᕽ ᐃᑕ
ᒫᓇ ᐁᐧᓴᐦᑫᒫᐦᑲᐧ ᑳ ᐋᓱᐊᐧᑳᒉ ᑲᐧᐢᑯᐦᑎᖬᐟ.

ᑫᑕᐦᑕᐁᐧ ᑕᑯᐦᑌᐤ ᐊᐊᐧ ᓈᐯᐤ ᑭᔮᐱᐣ
ᐁ ᐸᐦᐱᐦᐋᐧᐟ ᐱᖧᓯᓴ.

ᐅᑯᐢᑯᐦᐅᐁᐧᓴᐠ. ᐦᐊ. ᐁᓴᐩ. ᐋᐧᓴᑳᐨ ᓴᐯᕽ
ᑕᑯᐦᑌᐤ.

ᐦᐊ. ᒪᐦᑎ ᓂᑲ ᐋᓱᐊᐧᑳᒉ ᑲᐧᐢᑯᐦᑎᑊ.

ᓄᑳᑊ ᐁᓴ ᐊᓯᐦᑌᐤ ᐃᑲᐧ ᐃᑯᑌ ᐅᐦᒋ
ᐯᒋᐸᐦᑖᐤ. ᒉᐧᐦᒋ ᓴᐯᕽ ᐁ ᑕᑯᐸᐦᑖᐟ ᑳ ᓇᑫᐟ.

ᑫᑳᐣ ᐃᑌᐧᐤ ᐁᓴ ᑳ ᐋᐧᐸᒫᐟ ᐱᔭᐠ ᐱᖧᓯᓴ
ᐁ ᐅᐦᐸᐦᐅᖬᐟ ᓴᑳᖬᕽ ᐅᐦᒋ. ᑭᐦᑖᐧᐨ ᐊᓯᐦᑌᐤ
ᐃᑲᐧ ᒉᓇ ᐊᑎ ᓯᐯᐧᐸᐦᑖᐤ.

ᑫᑳᐣ ᐃᑌᐧᐤ ᐃᑲᐧ ᒉᓇ ᐁ ᓇᑫᐟ. ᐋᐧᐸᒉᐤ
ᓄᓱ ᐱᖧᓯᓴ ᐁ ᐅᐦᐸᐦᐅᖬᐟ ᓴᑳᖬᕽ ᐅᐦᒋ.
ᑭᐦᑖᐧᐨ ᐊᓯᐦᑌᐤ ᓇᐊᐧᐣ ᐃᑲᐧ ᐊᐧᐦᖬᐁᐧᐢ ᐅᐦᒋ
ᐊᑎ ᓯᐯᐧᐸᐦᑖᐤ.

ᑫᑳᐨ ᐃᑌᐧᐤ ᐁ ᓇᑫᐟ ᐃᑲᐧ ᒣᓇ. ᓂᐢᑐ ᐱᖧᓯᓴ ᐋᐧᐸᒣᐤ ᐁ ᐅᐦᐸᐦᐅᖨᐟ ᓴᑳᖨᕽ ᐅᐦᒋ. ᑭᐦᑖᐧᑦ ᐊᓯᐦᑌᐤ ᓇᐊᐧᐨ ᐊᐧᐦᖬᐁᐧᐣ ᐅᐦᒋ ᐊᑎ ᓯᐯᐧᐸᐦᑖᐤ. ᒣᐧᐦᒋ ᐁ ᐊᑎ ᑳᐧᐢᑯᐦᑎᐟ ᑳ ᓴᐢᒋ ᐅᐦᐸᐦᐅᖨᐟ ᒥᐦᒉᐟ ᐱᖧᐊᐧ. ᐊᐧᐦᐋᐧ. ᑲᐧᖬᐢᐠ ᑯᐢᑯᐃᐧᖨᐠ. ᒥᑐᓂ ᐁ ᐊᑎ ᐸᑲᐢᑕᐁᐧᓯᕽ ᓴᐯᕽ.

ᐅᑯᐢᑯᐦᐅᐁᐧᓴᐠ ᐅᑯᐢᑯᐦᐅᐁᐧᓴᐠ ᑳ ᐃᓯ ᐸᐦᐱᐦᐃᑯᐟ ᐁᓴ ᐊᓂᐦᐃ ᐅᑯᐢᑯᐦᐅᐁᐧᓴ.

ᐃᑳᐧᓂ ᐁ ᐃᐢᑳᐧᒋᒥᐦᒋᐠ ᐅᑯᐢᑯᐦᐅᐁᐧᓴᐠ.

(2) ᐊᐧᓂᓯᓇᐧᐠ ᓈᐯᓯᓴᐠ

ᑳᔮᐢ ᐆᒪ ᑳ ᑫ ᐊᐋᐧᓯᓴᐃᐧᔮᐣ ᒥᐦᒉᑖᐧᐤ ᒫᓇ ᓂᑫ ᓂᑕᐁᐧᖬᐦᒋᑳᓈᐣ ᓀᖬᓈᐣ ᓂᐢᑌᐢ ᐃᑲᐧ ᓂᓭᒥᐢ. ᐱᔭᑳᐧᐤ ᓂᑫ ᐊᐧᓂᓯᓂᓈᐣ. ᐊᐧᐦᐋ. ᑲᐧᔭᐢᐠ ᓂᑫ ᐊᐧᐋᐧᓀᖬᐦᑌᓈᐣ ᐊᖬᐢᐠ ᓂᑳᐁᐧᓈᐣ ᐁ ᑫ ᐃᑎᑯᔮᕽ ᑕ ᐯ ᑫᐁᐧᔮᕽ ᐊᑎ ᑎᐱᐢᑳᑭ.

ᐯ ᑫᐁᐧᐦᑫᐠ ᐊᑎ ᑎᐱᐢᑳᑭ ᑫ ᐃᑌᐧᐤ.

ᐋᐧᐦᐋᐧ. ᑖᓂᓯ ᒫᑲ ᑕ ᑫ ᐃᓯ ᐊᑎ ᑫᐁᐧᔮᕽ ᐁ ᒪᐧᔦ ᑎᐱᐢᑳᐠ. ᓂᐊᐧᓄᐦᑖᓈᐣ ᓴᑳᕽ.

ᐋᐢᑕᑦ ᐱᒥᑎᓴᐦᐅᐠ ᑳ ᐃᑌᐧᐟ ᓂᐢᑌᐢ. ᐃᔭᑯ ᐅᐢᑌᓯᒫᐤ ᒥᑖᑕᐦᐟ ᓀᓱᓵᑊ ᑫ ᐃᑕᐦᑐᐱᐳᓀᐤ. ᓂᐱᒥᑎᓴᐦᐋᐧᓈᐣ. ᑭᓀᐧᐢᐠ ᓂᐱᒥᑎᓴᐦᐋᐧᓈᐣ ᒫᑲ ᐋᐦᒋ ᐳᑯ ᓂᐊᐧᓂᓯᓂᓈᐣ. ᓇᐊᐧᐨ ᒥᐢᑕᐦᐃ ᓂᑕᑎ ᐊᐧᓂᓯᓂᓈᐣ.

ᐊᐊᐧᐢ. ᓀᖬ ᐃᑲᐧ ᓂᑲ ᓀᑳᓄᐦᑖᐣ ᓂᑎᑖᐧᐣ. ᒋᑰᒋ ᐁᐧᐸᐨ ᑭᑲ ᒪᑖᐃᐧᓯᓇᐤ ᓂᑎᓯ ᒪᒥᐦᒋᒧᐣ. ᒥᑖᑕᐦᐟ ᓀᖬ ᓂᑫ ᐃᑕᐦᑐᐱᐳᓈᐣ. ᑭᓀᐧᐢᐠ ᓂᑫ ᐱᒧᐦᑖᓈᐣ ᒫᑲ ᐋᐦᒋ ᐳᑯ ᓴᑳᕽ ᓂᑕᔮᓈᐣ. ᒥᑐᓂ ᐊᑎ ᐅᑖᑯᓯᐣ ᐁᐧᐸᐨ ᑕ ᐸᐦᑭᓯᒧᐣ. ᐯᖬᐢᐠ ᓂᓭᒥᐢ ᑳ ᐊᔭᒥᐟ.

ᒪᐦᑎ ᓀᖬ ᓂᑲ ᓀᑳᓄᐦᑖᐣ ᐃᑌᐧᐤ ᓂᓭᒥᐢ ᐁᐧᖬ ᐅᓭᒥᒫᐤ. ᓂᑲᓇᐋᐧᐸᒥᑐᓈᐣ ᓂᐢᑌᐢ ᐃᑲᐧ ᓀᖬ. ᓂᑫ ᐋᓂᐧᐦᑌᓈᐣ ᑕ ᑲᐢᑭᐦᑖᐟ ᑕ ᑫᐁᐧᐦᑕᐦᐃᑯᔮᕽ ᐊᖬᐢᐠ ᐊᖨᓈᓀᐤ ᐳᑯ ᐁ ᑫ ᐃᑕᐦᑐᐱᐳᓀᐟ. ᑭᔮᑦ ᓂᑕᑎ ᐱᒥᑎᓴᐦᐋᐧᓈᐣ. ᓇᒫᖬ ᑭᓀᐧᐢᐠ ᐃᐢᐯ ᑳ ᒪᑖᐃᐧᓯᔮᕽ ᐃᑕ ᑳ ᑫ ᑲᐯᓯᔮᕽ. ᒉᐧᐦᒋ ᐁ ᐊᑎ ᐸᐦᑭᓯᒧᐠ.

ᑭᔮᐱᐨ ᐊᓄᐦᐨ ᐁᐧᖬ ᓂᓭᒥᐢ ᓇᐊᐧᐨ ᓂᐦᑖ ᓂᑕᐁᐧᖬᐦᒋᑫᐤ. ᓇᒨᖬ ᐃᐧᐦᑳᐨ ᐊᐧᓂᓯᐣ.

(3) ᑲᔮᐢ ᑳ ᒪᑯᓭ ᑫᓯᑳᐠ

ᑲᔮᐢ ᒫᓇ ᐃᐢᐯ ᑳ ᒪᑯᓭ ᑫᓯᑳᐠ ᒥᑐᓂ ᒫᓇ ᐘᐦᔭᐤ ᐅᐦᒋ ᑫ ᐹ ᐯ ᐅᐦᑐᐦᑌᐦᐅᐘᐠ ᐊᔨᓯᑎᓂᐘᐠ ᑕ ᐯ ᐊᔭᒥᐦᐋᒋᐠ ᐆᑌ ᐋᒪᒋᐍᐢᐱᒍᐏᓂᕽ.

ᐘᐦᐚ ᑫ ᒫᐦ ᒨᒋᑭᐦᑖᑯᓯᐘᐠ ᒫᓇ ᐊᑎᒷᐠ ᑳ ᐱᒥᑎᓴᐦᐘᐢᑎᒸᐦᐅᐦᒋᐠ ᐊᔨᐢᐠ ᐁ ᑫ ᐘᐍᓭᐦᐅᐦᒋᐠ. ᓭᐍᐱᒋᑲᓂᓭ ᐅᑖᐹᓂᔮᐯᐚᕽ ᐁ ᐊᑯᑎᒥᒥᐦᐟ.

ᑭᐦᒋ ᐊᔭᒥᐦᐃᑭᒫᐤ ᒫᓇ ᐍᐢᑕ ᑫ ᐯ ᐅᑖᐸᐦᐊᐢᑎᒸᐤ ᑿᔭᐢᐠ ᑫ ᒫᐦ ᒥᔪᓯᐘᐠ ᐊᑎᒷᐠ.

ᒥᓯᐍᐢᑲᒥᐠ ᒫᓇ ᑫ ᐹ ᐯ ᐅᐦᑐᐦᑌᐦᐅᐘᐠ ᐊᔨᓯᑎᓂᐘᐠ ᐅᐘᐦᑰᒫᑲᓂᐚᐘ ᐁ ᐯ ᑳᐦ ᑭᔪᑲᐚᒋᐠ ᐃᑿ ᒉᓇ ᐁ ᐋᐩ ᐊᓱᑕᒫᑫᒋᐠ ᐅᒐᐚᓯᒥᓯᐚᐘ ᑕ ᐍᑭᐦᑐᔭᐟ ᐊᑎ ᓀᐱᓂᔭᑭ.

ᑫ ᒫᐦ ᒨᒋᑲᐣ. ᑳ ᑫᓯ ᐊᔭᒥᐦᐋᓂᐎᐠ ᑫ ᑳᐦ ᑭᔪᑳᑐᐘᐠ ᐊᔨᓯᑎᓂᐘᐠ. ᑫ ᐚᐦ ᐃᐦᑰᑫᐘᐠ ᐋᑎᐦᐟ ᑲᐦᑭᔭᐤ ᐊᐏᔭᐠ ᑫ ᒫᐦ ᒥᓯ ᒉᒥᓱᐤ. ᐋᑎᐦᐟ ᒉᓇ ᑫ ᒫ ᒉᐢᑯᒥ ᒉᔨᑐᐘᐠ ᒉᑭᐏᓇ.

ᑿᔭᐢᐠ ᐃᑯᐢᐯ ᑫ ᐋᐩ ᐃᑕᐦᑲᒥᑲᐣ.

(4) ᑯᐦᑯᒥᓈᓂᕽ

ᑲᔮᐢ ᐁᓴ ᒥᐢᑕᐦᐃ ᒫᓇ ᑫ ᐸᐹᒧᐦᑌᐦᐅᐊᐧᐠ
ᐃᔨᓂᐊᐧᐠ ᐁ ᓈ ᓂᑐᓇᐋᐧᒋᐠ ᐱᓯᐢᑭᐊᐧ
ᑕ ᐱᒫᑎᓯᐦᐃᓱᒋᐠ. ᐱᔭᑳᐧᐤ ᐁᓴ ᐁ ᑕᑳᐧᑭᓂᔨᐠ
ᐆᑯ ᐃᔨᓂᐊᐧᐠ ᐋᒪᒋᐁᐧᐢᐱᒧᐃᐧᓂᕽ ᐅᐦᒋ
ᑫ ᓯᐯᐧᐦᐅᐦᑌᐦᐅᐊᐧᐠ ᐃᑯᑕ ᐅᐦᒋ.

ᑫ ᐊᑎ ᑲᐯᓯᐊᐧᐠ ᓂᑭᑯ ᓵᑲᐦᐃᑲᓂᕽ ᐃᑯᑕ ᐱᔭᐠ
ᐁ ᒥᓵᔨᐠ ᐋᐧᓵᐤ ᑳ ᑫ ᒫᓄᑫᒋᐠ ᐱᔭᐠ ᑎᐱᐢᑳᐤ
ᐃᑯᑕ ᑫ ᐊᔮᐊᐧᐠ. ᑳ ᑫᑭᓭᐹᔮᔨᐠ ᐃᑕᓱᐁᐧᐊᐧᐠ
ᐁᓴ ᐅᐦᒋᑕᐤ ᐳᑯ ᑕ ᓇᑲᑖᒋᐠ ᐱᔭᐠ ᓅᒧᑫᐧᓯᐊᐧ
ᐅᓵᒼ ᑫᑳᐨ ᐁ ᑲᐃᐧᑭᐦᑳᔨᐟ ᐁ ᐸᐯᒣᔨᐟ
ᑳ ᒣᑳᐧ ᐱᒧᐦᑌᐦᐅᒋᐠ.

ᐃᑯᑕ ᐋᐧᓵᕽ ᓇᑲᑕᒪᐁᐧᐊᐧᐠ ᒣᒫᓂᐢ ᐃᑲᐧ ᑲᐦᑭᔭᐤ
ᐅᑖᐸᒋᐦᒋᑲᓇ. ᓇᒨᔭ ᓈᓂᑕᐤ ᐅᐦᒋ ᐃᑌᔨᐦᑕᒼ
ᐊᐊᐧ ᓅᒧᑫᐧᓯᐤ ᐅᐦᒋᑕᐤ ᒫᓇ ᐃᑯᓯ
ᐁ ᑫ ᐃᑑᑕᐦᑳᐧᐤ ᑲᔮᐢ ᐃᔨᓂᐊᐧᐠ.

ᐱᔭᑳᐧᐤ ᐁᓴ ᐁ ᐅᑖᑯᓯᓂᔨᐠ ᑳ ᐋᐧᐸᒫᐟ ᒨᓴᐧ
ᐊᐊᐧ ᓅᒧᑫᐧᓯᐤ ᐁ ᐋᓱᐊᐧᐦᐊᒥᔨᐟ ᓵᑲᐦᐃᑲᐣ.
ᐦᐊᐩ. ᑫᓯᐢᑲᐤ ᐴᓯᐸᔨᐦᐅᐤ ᒣᒫᓂᓯᕽ ᐁ ᑕᐦᑯᓈᕽ
ᐯᒥᓇᐦᑳᐧᐣ ᐃᑲᐧ ᒣᑲᐦᐃᑲᓂᐢ ᐁ ᓇᐊᐧᓵᐧᑖᐟ ᐊᓂᐦᐃ
ᒨᓴᐧ. ᐦᐊᐩ. ᑲᐢᑭᐦᑖᐤ ᑕ ᑖᐸᑳᐧᑖᐟ ᐃᑲᐧ
ᐃᑯᑕ ᐅᐦᒋ ᐊᑎ ᒣᑲᐦᐁᐧᐤ ᐅᐢᑎᑳᐧᓂᔨᕽ. ᑲᐧᔭᐢᐠ
ᓀᐯᑲᐧᐦᐃᓱᐤ.

ᑳ ᓭᑲᐧᓂᖪᐠ ᐁᓴ ᐅᐋᐧᐦᑰᒫᑲᓇ ᑳᐃᐧ ᑕᑯᐦᑌᐦᐅᖪᐊᐧ
ᐃᑯᑕ ᒥᐢᑳᑯᐤ ᑮᔪᐱᐨ ᐁ ᒪ ᒣᒋᖪᐟ ᑳᐢᑫᐊᐧᐠ
ᑲᐯ ᐱᐳᐣ ᐁᓴ ᐁ ᒫᐦ ᒨᐋᐧᐟ ᐊᓂᐦᐃ ᒨᓴᐧ
ᑳ ᑫ ᓂᐸᐦᐋᐧᐟ.

ᐃᑯᐢᐯ ᐅᐦᒋ ᑯᐦᑯᒥᓈᓂᕽ ᐯ ᐃᒋᑳᑌᐤ ᐃᔪᑯ
ᐋᐧᓵᐤ ᐃᑕ ᑳ ᑫ ᐱᔪᑯ ᐱᐳᓂᓯᐟ ᐊᐊᐧ ᓅᒍᑫᐧᓯᐤ.

OUT OF
ORDER
HM 2013

(5) *Shaking-Spear* ᐸᐹᒧᐦᑌᐤ

ᐱᔭᑳᐧᐤ ᐁᓴ *Shaking Spear* ᐸ ᐱᒧᐦᑌᐤ ᒣᐢᑲᓈᕽ. ᐋᐧᐸᒣᐤ ᒧᐢᑐᓴᐧ.

ᑖᓂᓯ ᐃᑌᐧᐤ ᐊᐊᐧ ᓈᐯᐤ.

ᒨᐤ ᒨᐤ ᐃᑌᐧᐤ ᐊᐊᐧ ᐱᔭᐠ ᒧᐢᑐᐢ. ᑯᐢᑯᐦᑕᐁᐧᐤ ᐆᐦᐅ ᒧᐢᑐᓴᐧ *Shaking-Spear!*

ᐦᐊᐩ ᐊᐊᐧᐢ ᓇᒨᔭ ᓂᓇᐦᑌ ᐲᒥᓲᐣ ᐃᑌᐧᐤ ᐊᐊᐧ *Shaking-Spear.*

ᓵᓴᐩ ᒣᓇ ᐱᒧᐦᑌᐤ ᒣᐢᑲᓈᕽ *Shaking-Spear.* ᐋᐧᐸᒣᐤ ᒫᔭᒥᐦᑯᓴ.

ᑖᓂᓯ ᑳ ᐃᑖᐟ ᐁᓴ ᐆᐦᐅ ᒫᔭᒥᐦᑯᓴ.

ᐹ ᐹ ᑳ ᐃᑎᑯᐟ ᐱᔭᐠ ᒫᔭᒥᐦᑯᓴ. ᐊᐧᐦᐋᐧ. ᑯᐢᑯᐦᑕᐁᐧᐤ.

ᐦᐊᐩ ᐊᐊᐧᐢ. ᓇᒨᔭ ᓄᔭ ᑭᐹᐹ ᑳ ᐃᑖᐟ ᐁᓴ. ᐊᑎ ᓯᐯᐧᐦᑌᐤ. ᑲᐧᔭᐢᐠ ᑭᓯᐋᐧᓯᐤ.

ᓵᓴᐩ ᒣᓇ ᐱᒧᐦᑌᐤ ᒣᐢᑲᓈᕽ *Shaking-Spear.* ᐃᐢᐸᑎᓈᕽ ᐋᐧᐸᒣᐤ ᒥᐢᑎᑲᐧ. ᒫᑐᐤ ᐁᓴ ᐊᐊᐧ ᒥᐢᑎᐠ.

ᑖᓄᐦᑭ ᑳ ᒫᑐᔭᐣ ᐃᓯ ᑲᑫᐧᒥᒣᐤ ᐆᐦᐅ ᒥᐢᑎᑲᐧ.

ᐊᔨᐢᐠ ᑕᐦᑐ ᑫᓯᑳᐤ ᐊᐘ ᐱᔭᐠ ᐊᑎᒼ ᐁ ᓯᑭᓯᐟ ᑳ ᐃᓯ ᒨᑐᐟ ᐊᐘ ᒥᐢᑎᐠ. ᑭᑎᒫᑭᐦᑕᐍᐤ ᐆᐦᐅ ᒥᐢᑎᑿ.

ᐦᐊᐤ ᒉᐢᑿ ᑭᑲ ᐍᒋᐦᐃᑎᐣ ᐃᑘᐤ ᐁᓴ ᐊᐘ ᓈᐯᐤ. ᐊᑎ ᒪᓯᓇᐦᐃᑫᐤ.

ᐊᑎ ᓯᐻᐦᑌᐤ *Shaking-Spear.* ᒋᐦᑫᔨᐦᑕᒼ ᐊᔨᐢᐠ ᐁ ᐍᒋᐦᐚᐟ ᒥᐢᑎᑿ.

ᒣᐧᐢᒐᒌᐢ ᐁᓴ ᐯ ᑕᑯᐦᑌᐤ ᐊᐘ ᐊᑎᒼ. ᐘᐦᐚ ᑯᐢᑵᐱᓯᐣ. ᐊᔭᒥᐦᑖᐤ ᐊᓂᒪ ᑳ ᑫ ᒪᓯᓇᐦᐊᕽ *Shaking-Spear: "Out of Order"* ᐁ ᐃᑕᐢᑌᔨᐠ. ᐁᑵᓂ ᓇᒨᔭ ᑲᐢᑭᐦᑖᐤ ᑕ ᓯᑭᐟ. ᐊᑎ ᓯᐻᐦᑌᐤ. ᑭᓯᐚᓯᐤ.

ᑿᔭᐢᐠ ᒋᐦᑫᔨᐦᑕᒼ ᐊᐘ ᒥᐢᑎᐠ.

HM2013

(6) *Shaking-Spear* ᐃᑲᐧ ᒪᐢᑲᐧ

ᐱᔭᑳᐧᐤ ᐁ ᓀᐱᓂᔨᐠ *Shaking-Spear* ᑫ ᓄᐦᑌ ᓂᑕᐃᐧᒥᓀᐤ. ᑫ ᐱᐦᑕᒼ ᐁ ᒥᐦᒉᑎᓂᔨᑭ ᐃᔨᓂᒥᓇ ᐊᓄᐦᐨ ᑳ ᓀᐱᓂᔨᐠ. ᐃᑳᐧᓂ ᑯᐢᐱᐤ. ᑕᑲᐦᑭ ᑫᓯᑳᔨᐤ.

ᑭᓀᐧᓴᐢ ᓄᐦᒋᒥᕽ ᓴᑳᕽ ᐸ ᐱᒧᐦᑌᐤ ᐁ ᐊᓴᐋᐧᐊᐦᑕᕽ ᒣᓂᓴ. ᓇᒨᔭ ᐅᓵᒼ ᒥᐢᑕᐦᐃ ᒥᐢᑲᒼ. ᑳ ᑭᐢᑭᓯᐟ ᐃᑌ ᒫᓇ ᑳ ᑫ ᓂᑕᐃᐧᒥᓀᒋᐠ ᐃᐢᐯ ᑳ ᑫ ᐊᐋᐧᓯᓴᐃᐧᐟ ᓇᒨᔭ ᐅᓵᒼ ᐊᐧᐦᔨᐤ ᐃᑕ ᐅᐦᒋ ᑳ ᐱᒧᐦᑌᐟ ᒫᑲ ᐅᐦᒋᑕᐤ ᐳᑯ ᑕ ᐋᒪᒋᐁᐧᐟ ᐊᐧᒋᐩ.

ᐃᑳᐧᓂ ᑕᑯᐦᑌᐤ ᐃᑕ ᐅᐦᒋ ᑕ ᐊᑎ ᒫᒋ ᐋᒪᒋᐁᐧᐟ ᐊᐧᒋᐩ. ᓂᓯᐦᑳᐨ ᐊᑎ ᐋᐩ ᐋᒪᒋᐁᐧᐤ ᐋᐢᑲᐤ ᒫᓇ ᐋᐧᐸᐦᑕᒼ ᒣᓂᓴ ᐃᔭᑯᓂ ᐊᑎ ᒫᐦ ᒨᒥᓀᐤ. ᐯᔨᐢᐠ ᑕᐦᑯᐦᑖᒪᑎᐣ ᑕᑯᐦᑌᐤ. ᐃᑯᑕ ᐅᐦᒋ ᐊᓴᐋᐧᐱᐤ. ᐊᐧᐦᐋᐧ. ᒨᒋᑳᐱᓯᐣ. ᑲᐧᔭᐢᐠ ᒥᓯᐁᐧᑕ ᐁ ᓴᐱᐦᑳᐧᔨᐠ ᐃᔨᑯᕽ ᐁ ᒣᓂᓯᐢᑳᔨᐠ. ᒨᒋᑫᔨᐦᑕᒼ. ᐃᑯᑕ ᓴᒫᐠ ᓇᐦᐊᐱᐸᔨᐦᐅᐤ ᐁ ᐊᑎ ᒪᐃᐧᓱᐟ ᐃᑲᐧ ᒣᓇ ᐋᐢᑲᐤ ᐁ ᒫᐦ ᒨᒥᓀᓯᐟ.

ᒥᑐᓂ ᑭᓀᐧᓴᐢ ᒪ ᒪᐃᐧᓱᐤ ᐅᓵᒼ ᐁ ᐅᑕᒣᔨᐟ ᓇᒫᐧᐨ ᓈᑲᑕᐁᐧᔨᐦᑕᒼ ᐆᒪ ᐃᑕ ᑳ ᐊᔮᐟ. ᑫᑕᐦᑕᐁᐧ ᑳ ᐱᐦᑕᐋᐧᐟ ᐊᐃᐧᔭ ᐁ ᐱᒪᐦᑲᒥᑭᓯᔨᐟ ᑭᐦᒋᐋᐧᐠ ᐃᑕ ᐊᐊᐧ ᑳ ᒪᐃᐧᓱᐟ. ᑫᓯᐢᑲᐤ ᐊᓴᐋᐧᐱᐤ. ᐊᐧᐦᐋᐧ. ᐋᐧᐸᒣᐤ ᒪᐢᑲᐧ ᐁ ᒪᑌᐧ ᒨᒥᓀᔨᐟ. ᑫᓯᐢᑲᐤ ᑳᓲᐸᔨᐦᐅᐤ ᐊᐊᐧ

ᓈᐯᐤ. ᑯᐢᑌᐤ ᐆᐦᐅ ᒪᐢᑿ. ᓂᓯᐦᑳᐨ ᐊᑎ ᓯᐍᐦᑌᐤ ᐃᑯᑕ ᐅᐦᒋ. ᐘᐦᐋ. ᐚᐸᒥᑯᐤ ᐆᐦᐅ ᒪᐢᑿ.

ᑿᐦᒋᐸᐦᑖᐤ ᐃᑯᑕ ᐅᐦᒋ ᐊᐘ ᓈᐯᐤ ᐁ ᓇᑲᒋᐸᐦᑖᐟ ᐅᒪᐏᓱᐏᐣ. ᐍᐢᑕ ᒪᐢᑿ ᑿᐦᒋᐸᐦᑖᐤ ᐁ ᐊᑎ ᓇᐘᓵᐧᑖᐟ ᐆᐦᐅ ᓈᐯᐘ. ᑿᔭᐢᐠ ᓴᑭᓯᐤ ᐊᐘ ᓈᐯᐤ.

ᐃᒁᓂ ᐊᑎ ᓂᐦᑕᒋᐍᐸᐦᑖᐤ ᐅᐓ ᓈᐯᐤ. ᐍᐢᑕ ᒪᐢᑿ ᐊᑎ ᑲᑵ ᓂᐦᑕᒋᐍᐸᐦᑖᐤ. ᐦᐊᐩ. ᐊᑎ ᑖᐦ ᑌᐻᐤ *Shaking-Spear* ᐃᔨᑯᕽ ᐁ ᓴᑭᓯᐟ. ᐱᐦᑕᐍᐤ ᐆᐦᐅ ᒪᐢᑿ ᑖᐱᐢᑰᐨ ᐍᐸᐨ ᐁ ᐍ ᐅᑎᐦᑎᐦᐃᑯᐟ. ᐦᐊᐩ. ᑿᔭᐢᐠ ᑭᓭᐍᐤ ᐊᐘ ᒫᐢᑿ ᑖᐱᐢᑰᐨ ᐁ ᒪᐦ ᒪᑘᓯᕽ ᓴᑳᕽ ᓇᐘᐨ ᑭᐦᒋᐚᐠ ᐁ ᐯ ᐱᐦᑖᑯᓯᔨᐟ. ᑫᑕᐦᑕᐍ ᑳ ᐚᐸᒫᐟ *Shaking-Spear* ᐆᐦᐅ ᒪᐢᑿ ᐁ ᒥᔮᐢᑳᑯᐟ. ᐁ ᐯ ᓂᐦᑕᒋᐍ ᑎᐦᑎᐯᐸᔨᔨᐟ ᐁᓴ.

ᑭᐱᐦᒉᐤ *Shaking-Spear* ᐁ ᐊᑎ ᐅᓵᒥ ᐸᐦᐱᐦᐋᐟ ᐊᓂᐦᐃ ᒪᐢᑿ.

(7) ᐸᐢᑳᐧᐃᐧ ᒧᐢᑐᐢ ᒥᑕᐦᑕᐦᑲᐧᓇ

ᑲᔮᐢ ᑭᒧᓲᒥᐸᓂᓇᐘᐠ ᑫ ᓂᐦᑖ ᒫᒉᐘᐠ. ᒉᐢᐟ ᓂᐍ ᐚᒋᒫᐘᐠ ᐆᑯ. ᐃᐧᐦᑳᐨ ᓈ ᑭᒉᒥᐟ ᐊᓂᐦᐃ ᒉᒥᐃᐧᓂᓴ *Buffalo Wings* ᑳ ᐃᒋᑳᑌᑭ. ᐸᐢᑳᐧᐃᐧ ᒧᐢᑐᐢ ᒥᑕᐦᑕᐦᑲᐧᓇ ᐊᓂᐦᐃ ᐃᐧᐦᑲᓯᓇᐧ ᒫᓇ ᐃᔭᑯᓂ.

ᐦᐊᐤ ᑲ ᐃᐧᐦᑕᒫᑎᐟ. ᑲᔮᐢ ᒫᓇ ᐃᐢᐯ ᑐᐦᐃᖬᐘᐠ ᑳ ᑫ ᓅᒋᐦᐋᒋᐠ ᐸᐢᑳᐧᐃᐧ ᒧᐢᑐᓴᐧ ᓇᒨᖬ ᒫᓇ ᑲᑖᐨ ᑫ ᐁᐧ ᓂᐸᐦᐁᐘᐠ ᑌᐱᖬᕽ ᒫᓇ ᐅᑕᐦᑕᐦᑲᐧᓂᐋᐧᐊᐧ ᐁ ᑫ ᓈᑖᐧᑕᐦᑕᐦᑲᐧᓂᐦᐋᐧᒋᐠ ᐃᖪᑯᕽ ᐁ ᑫ ᓇᐦᐁᒋᐠ. ᑖᐯᐧ. ᐁ ᑫᑲᐢᑭᑕᐦᑕᐦᑲᐧᓂᐦᐋᐧᒋᐠ ᒫᓇ ᐳᑯ ᐆᐦᐅ ᐸᐢᑳᐧᐃᐧ ᒧᐢᑐᓴᐧ ᐸᐢᑳᐧᐃᐧ ᒧᐢᑐᐢ ᒥᑕᐦᑕᐦᑲᐧᓇ ᐁᐧᐢᑕᐋᐧᐤ ᐁ ᑫ ᐃᐧᐦᑭᐢᑕᐦᑳᐧᐤ.

ᑳᖪᑎᐧᕽ ᑫ ᓈᐦ ᓇᐦᐁᐘᐠ. ᓇᒨᖬ ᒫᐧᓯ ᑫ ᓈᐦ ᓂᐸᐦᐁᐘᐠ ᐊᓂᐦᐃ ᐸᐢᑳᐧᐃᐧ ᒧᐢᑐᓴᐧ. ᐯᖪᐢᐠ ᑫ ᐊᑎ ᒥᐦᒉᑎᐘᐠ ᐆᑯ ᐸᐢᑳᐧᐃᐧ ᒧᐢᑐᓴᐧᐠ ᐯᖪᐢᐠ ᐊᑎ ᓈᐦ ᓂᐦᑖᐃᐧᑭᐘᐠ ᐸᐢᑳᐧᐃᐧ ᒧᐢᒍᓯᓯᓴᐠ ᐁᑳ ᐊᐘᓯᒉ ᐁ ᐅᑕᐦᑕᐦᑲᐧᓂᒋᐠ *evolution* ᐅᐦᒋ ᐃᔭᑯ ᐅᐦᒋ *evolution* ᑳ ᐃᒋᑳᑌᐠ. ᐁᔭᑯ ᐅᐦᒋ ᐊᓄᐦᐨ ᐁᑳ ᐊᐘᓯᒉ ᐁ ᐅᑕᐦᑕᐦᑲᐧᓂᒋᐠ ᐆᑯ ᐸᐢᑳᐧᐃᐧ ᒧᐢᑐᓴᐧᐠ ᑖᐯᐧ ᐊᓂᒪ. ᑲᐧᔭᐢᐠ ᑫ ᓈᐦ ᓇᐦᐁᐘᐠ ᑲᔮᐢ ᑭᒧᓲᒥᐸᓂᓇᐘᐠ.

ᒥᑐᓂ ᑭ ᐊᑎ ᐅᓵᒥᔭᑕᐘᐠ ᐆᑌ ᐸᐢᑲᐧᕽ ᐆᑯ ᐸᐢᑳᐧᐃᐧ ᒧᐢᑐᓴᐧᐠ ᐁᑳ ᐊᐘᓯᒉ ᐁ ᐅᑕᐦᑕᐦᑲᐧᓂᒋᐠ ᐃᔭᑯ ᐅᐦᒋ ᐆᒪ ᐃᐢᐯ ᑳ ᑕᑯᐦᑌᐦᐅᒋᐠ ᐊᑳᒪᐢᑭᕽ

ᐅᐦᒋ ᐊᖬᓯᑎᓂᐊᐧᐠ ᐆᑯ ᒨᓂᔮᐊᐧᐠ ᓇᒫᐧᐨ
ᐁᐧᖬᐋᐧᐤ ᐅᐦᒋ ᐋᐧᐸᒣᐊᐧᐠ ᐸᐢᑳᐧᐃᐧ ᒧᐢᑐᓴᐧ
ᐁ ᐅᑕᐦᑕᐦᑲᐧᓂᖬᐟ.

ᒫᒪᐢᑳᐨ ᒫᑲ ᐆᑯ ᒪᒪᐦᑖᐃᐧᓯᐊᐧᐠ. ᑭᔮᐱᐨ
ᐹᐦ ᐱᒥᓇᐊᐧᓱᐊᐧᐠ ᒣᓇ ᐊᑖᐋᐧᑫᐊᐧᐠ ᐆᐦᐅ
ᐸᐢᑳᐧᐃᐧ ᒧᐢᑐᐢ ᒥᑕᐦᑕᐦᑲᐧᓇ.

ᑖᐯᐧ ᐃᐧᐦᑲᓯᓇᐧ.

(8) ᒍᐦᒍᐦᑳᓯᐃᐧᐣ

ᐱᔭᑳᐧᐤ ᐁ ᑫ ᒫᑎᓈᐃᐧ ᑫᓯᑳᐠ ᓂᑫ ᓄᐦᑌ ᐃᐢᐸᔨᐣ ᑭᐦᒋ ᒎᐦᑯᒫᓇᐢᑫᕽ ᐊᔨᐢᐠ ᐁ ᑫᐧᑕ ᐱᐦᑖᐧᔮᐣ. ᓂᑫ ᓂᑕᐁᐧᔨᒫᐊᐧᐠ ᓯᑲᕒᐁᑎᓭᐠ ᑭᐦᒋ ᒎᐦᑯᒫᓂᓈᕽ ᐅᐦᒋ ᐊᔨᐢᐠ ᐃᔭᑯᓂᐠ ᓇᐊᐧᐨ ᐁ ᑕᑲᐦᑭᐢᐸᑯᓯᒥᐠ ᐃᔨᑯᕽ ᐆᑕ ᐅᐦᒋ ᑭᑕᐢᑫᓈᕽ ᑳᓇᑖᕽ.

ᐃᑳᐧᓂ ᐁᐧᐸᐨ ᐁ ᑫᑭᓴᐹᔮᐠ ᓂᑫ ᓯᐯᐧᐸᔨᐣ. ᓂᑫ ᐱᔭᑯᐦᑫᐣ. ᓀᑳᐣ ᐱᑕᒫ ᓂᑫ ᐱᐦᒥᐱᒫᐣ ᐃᑲᐧ ᒣᓇ ᐱᐦᑲᑌᐋᐧᐳᐩ ᑎᒣᓯᕽ ᓂᑫ ᐊᑖᐁᐧᐢᑕᒫᓱᐣ. ᐃᑳᐧᓂ ᓂᑫ ᓯᐯᐧᑯᒋᓂᐣ.

ᐃᐢᐯ ᑳ ᑕᑯᐸᔨᔮᐣ ᑎᐸᐦᐊᐢᑳᓂᕽ ᒫᑲ ᒣᓇ ᓂᑲᑫᐧᒋᒥᑲᐃᐧᐣ ᑖᓂᑌ ᐁ ᐁᐧ ᐃᐢᐸᔨᔮᐣ ᐃᑲᐧ ᒣᓇ ᑫᐢᐱᐣ ᑭᓄᐧᐢᐠ ᐃᑯᑌ ᐁ ᐁᐧ ᐱᒪᐦᑲᒥᑭᓯᔮᐣ. ᓂᐃᐧᐦᑕᒪᐋᐧᐊᐧᐠ ᑎᐸᐦᐊᐢᑳᐣ ᑫᑌᔨᐦᑕᒫᐊᐧᓱᐊᐧᐠ ᑌᐱᔭᕽ *Plenty*ᐅᐧᑎᕽ ᑳ ᐁᐧ ᐃᐢᐸᔨᔮᐣ ᐃᑲᐧ ᒣᓇ ᑲᓇᑫ ᐱᔭᐠ ᑫᓯᑳᐤ ᑳ ᐁᐧ ᐱᒪᐦᑲᒥᑭᓯᔮᐣ ᐃᑯᑌ. ᓂᐸᑭᑎᓂᑲᐧᐠ ᑕ ᐊᑳᒥ ᑎᐸᐦᐊᐢᑳᓂᓯᔮᐣ.

ᓇᒎᔭ ᑭᓄᐧᐢᐠ ᐃᐢᐯ ᑳ ᑕᑯᐸᔨᔮᐣ *Plenty*ᐅᐧᑎᕽ. ᓂᑭᐱᐦᒋᐸᔨᐣ ᐊᑖᐃᐧᑲᒥᑯᕽ ᐃᑲᐧ ᐃᑯᑕ ᓂᑕᑖᐁᐧᐢᑕᒫᓱᐣ ᐱᔭᑳᐧᔪᕽ ᓯᑲᕒᐁᑎᓭᐠ ᐃᑲᐧ ᒣᓇ ᓂᑕᑖᐁᐧᐢᑕᒪᐋᐧᐤ ᓂᑑᑌᑦ ᓲᒥᓈᐳᐩ. ᑳ ᐴᓈᐦᑲᒥᑭᓯᔮᐣ ᐊᑖᐃᐧᑲᒥᑯᕽ ᓂᓂᑐᓀᐣ ᓈᓂᑕᐤ ᐃᑕ ᑕ ᒣᒋᓲᔮᐣ ᓂᓯᐦᑳᐨ ᓂᐱᒪᑯᒋᓂᐣ ᑫᑕᐦᑕᐁᐧ ᑳ ᐋᐧᐸᐦᑕᒫᐣ *"Harvest Moon Casino".* ᓴᒫᐠ ᐁᑯᑕ ᓂᑭᐱᐦᒫᐣ ᐁ ᐁᐧ ᓂᑕᐃᐧ ᑲᑫᐧ ᐅᑕᐦᐃᑫᔮᐣ ᒥᐢᑕᐦᐃ ᓲᓂᔮᐤ ᓇᒎᔭ ᐊᐦᔫ ᓂᑫ ᐅᐦᒋ ᒣᒋᓱᐣ.

ᑭᓄᐧᐢᐠ ᐃᑯᑕ ᐱᐦᒑᔭᕽ ᑲᓭᓅᕽ ᓂᒫᖪᖬᐦᒥᑳᐣ ᐋᐢᑲᐤ ᓂᑐᑕᐦᐃᑳᐠ ᒫᑲ ᓇᐊᐧᐨ ᒥᐢᑕᐦᐃ ᓰᓂᔮᐤ ᓂᐊᐧᓂᐦᐋᐤ ᐯᖬᐢᐠ ᓂᑕᑎ ᒉᐢᒐᐦᐅᑲᐃᐧᐣ. ᐊᐧᐦᐋᐧ ᒥᐢᑕᐦᐃ ᓂᐯᑫᐧᖬᐦᑌᐣ ᐃᐢᐯ ᑳᐃᐧ ᑳ ᐆᓯᔮᐣ ᓂᑐᑖᐸᓈᐢᑯᕽ. ᓂᑭᑖᐸᐦᑌᐣ ᐃᖪᑯᕽ ᐱᒥᐩ ᑳ ᐊᔮᔮᐣ ᐃᔭᐤ. ᐊᑳᐋᐧᐨ ᐁᑐᑫ ᓂᑲ ᑕᑯᐸᖬᐣ ᓄᑭᕽ ᒥᖪᐸᖬᐦᐃᑯᔮᓂ ᐅᑎ. ᓇᒪ ᑫᑲᐧᐩ ᓂᑐᓰᓂᔮᒥᐣ ᐊᖬᐢᐠ ᐁ ᑫ ᒉᐢᒐᐦᐅᑲᐃᐧᔮᐣ ᐃᑳᐧᓂ ᓇᒨᖭ ᓂᑲᐢᑭᐦᑖᐣ ᑕ ᐊᑖᐁᐧᐢᑕᒫᓰᔮᐣ ᐱᒥᐩ. ᓂᓯᐦᑳᐨ ᓂᑕᑎ ᑫᐁᐧᑯᒥᓂᐣ. ᓇᒨᖭ ᑭᓄᐧᐢᐠ ᑳ ᓇᑲᑕᒫᐣ ᑎᐸᐦᐊᐢᑳᐣ ᐃᐢᐯ ᓵᓴᐩ ᑳ ᐃᓯᓈᑲᐧᕽ ᐁ ᐊᑎ ᒉᐢᒥᐱᒥᔮᐣ.

ᓂᑕᑎ ᒫᐦ ᒪᐃᐧᒧᓯᐣ.

ᐃᐢᐸᖬᐦᐃᑯᔮᓂ ᑕ ᑌᐱᐸᖬᐦᐃᑯᔮᐠ ᐱᒥᐩ ᓄᑭᕽ ᐃᐢᑯ ᓇᒪ ᐃᐧᐦᑳᐨ ᑭᐦᑖᐧᑦ ᓂᑲ ᒫᖪᖬᐦᑌᐣ ᑲᓭᓄᐤ. ᐃᑯᓯ ᓂᑎᓯ ᒪᐃᐧᒧᓯᐣ. ᑫᑕᐦᑕᐁᐧ ᑳ ᐱᐢᑕᐦᐊᐧᐠ ᓯᑳᐠ ᐊᐧᐦᐋᐧ ᑲᐧᔭᐢᐠ ᐃᐧᐦᒉᑭᓯᐤ ᓂᑐᑖᐸᓈᐢᑲᑦ.

ᒫᒪᐢᑳᐨ ᓂᑎᑖᐧᐣ ᐃᑲᐧ ᓂᑕᑎ ᐋᑳᖭᓴᒧᐣ *"God, I needed gas but not that kind of gas."*

ᒫᒪᐢᑳᐨ ᒫᓂ ᒫᑲ ᓂᑫ ᐊᑎ ᒥᖪᐸᖬᐦᐃᑲᐣ ᑲᒥᐢᑲᐤ ᓄᑭᕽ ᐁ ᑕᑯᐸᖭᔮᐣ ᐃᐢᐯ ᑳ ᒉᐢᒥᐱᒉᐸᖭᔮᐣ.

HM'13

(9) ᐱᓯᐢᑭᐊᐧᐠ ᐅᑑᑌᒥᑐᐊᐧᐠ

ᑲᔮᐢ ᐁᓴ ᑫ ᐸ ᐱᔭᑯᐊᐧᐠ ᐆᑯ ᐱᓯᐢᑭᐊᐧᐠ. ᑲᐧᔭᐢᐠ ᐁᓴ ᐊᐊᐧ ᐱᔭᐠ ᐋᐸᑯᓯᐢ ᑫ ᑭᑎᒫᑫᔨᒥᓱᐤ.

ᒪᑖᐧᐣ ᒉ ᓈᓂᑕᐤ ᐃᑌ ᓂᑐᑑᑌᒥᐣ ᐃᑌᔨᐦᑕᒼ ᐁᓴ. ᒪᐦᑎ ᓂᐁᐧ ᓂᑕᐃᐧ ᓂᑐᓇᐋᐧᐊᐧᐠ ᐃᑌᐧ ᐁᓴ. ᐃᑳᐧᓂ ᐊᑎ ᓯᐯᐧᐦᑌᐤ. ᑭᓀᐧᐢᐠ ᐸ ᐱᒧᐦᑌᐤ ᐊᐊᐧ ᐋᐸᑯᓯᐢ. ᑫᑕᐦᑕᐁᐧ ᐁᓴ ᐊᐃᐧᔭ ᓇᑭᐢᑲᐁᐧᐤ.

ᓇᐊᐧᐨ ᐳᑯ ᐊᐧᐃᐧᔭᓯᓇᐁᐧᐤ ᐆᐦᐅ ᐊᔭᐦᒋ ᐱᓯᐢᑭᐊᐧ ᐊᔨᐢᐠ ᐁ ᑭᓄᐦᑕᐊᐧᑫᔨᐟ. ᐸ ᐱᔭᐦᑕᐠ ᐆᑯ ᓀᓱ ᐱᓯᐢᑭᐊᐧᐠ ᑲ ᑭᑖᐸᒥᑐᐊᐧᐠ ᐁ ᐊᐧ ᐋᐧᐢᑳᑎᑖᑐᒋᐠ ᒫᑲ ᐯᔨᐢᐠ ᑭᓯᐋᐧᐠ ᐊᑎ ᓈᑎᑐᐊᐧᐠ. ᑳᐦ ᑲᑫᐧᒋᒥᑐᐊᐧᐠ.

ᐊᐁᐧᓇ ᐆᒪ ᑫᔭ ᐃᑌᐧᐤ ᐊᐊᐧ ᐋᐸᑯᓯᐢ.

ᐋᐧᐳᐢ ᒫᓇ ᓂᑎᑎᑲᐃᐧᐣ ᐃᑌᐧᐤ ᐊᐊᐧ ᑭᓄᐦᒐᐊᐧᑳᐢ ᐊᐊᐧ ᐊᔭᐦᒋ ᐱᓯᐢᑭᐤ. ᑫᔭ ᒫᑲ ᐊᐁᐧᓇ ᐆᒪ ᑫᔭ.

ᐋᐸᑯᓯᐢ ᐆᒪ ᓀᔭ ᐃᑌᐧᐤ ᐊᐊᐧ ᐋᐸᑯᓯᐢ. ᑭᓄᐦᑌ ᐅᑑᑌᒥᒥᐣ ᓈ.

ᐦᐊᐤ ᑖᐯᐧ ᐃᑌᐧᐤ ᐊᐊᐧ ᐋᐧᐳᐢ ᐁᐧᐢᑕ ᐊᔨᐢᐠ ᐁ ᑫ ᐸ ᐱᔭᑯᐟ ᐃᑲᐧ ᐁᐧᐢᑕ ᐊᐃᐧᔭ ᐁ ᑫ ᓄᐦᑌ ᐅᑑᑌᒥᐟ.

ᐃᑳᐧᓂ ᐊᑎ ᐅᑑᑌᒥᑐᐊᐧᐠ. ᐊᑎ ᐱᒧᐦᑌᐊᐧᐠ ᒣᐢᑲᓈᕽ. ᑫᑕᐦᑕᐁᐧ ᐋᐧᐸᒣᐊᐧᐠ ᐊᐃᐧᔭ ᐁ ᐱᒧᐦᑌᖨᐟ ᒣᐢᑲᓈᕽ ᐁ ᓀᑳᓀᐢᑳᑯᒥᐠ. ᓵᑳᓯᕽ ᑳᔨᒨᐸᖨᐦᐅᐊᐧᐠ ᐃᑯᑕ ᐅᐦᒋ ᐁ ᑲᓇᐚᐸᒫᒋᐠ ᐆᐦᐅ ᐊᔭᐦᒋ ᐱᓯᐢᑭᐊᐧ. ᒫᒪᐢᑳᑌᐊᐧᐠ ᐃᑲᐧ ᐊᑎ ᑭᑎᒫᑫᓇᐃᐧᐊᐧᐠ ᐊᖨᐢᐠ ᐁ ᓀᔨᑳᑌᖨᐟ ᐳᑯ ᐃᑲᐧ ᒣᓇ ᑲᒥᐢᑲᐤ ᐁ ᐅᐯᐚᖨᐟ. ᓵᑭᐢᑫᐧᐊᐧᐠ ᐆᑯ ᓀᔨ ᐱᓯᐢᑭᐊᐧᐠ ᐁ ᐊᑎ ᔨᐦᑭᑌᐦᐁᒋᐠ ᐃᑲᐧ ᐊᑎ ᐊᔭᒥᐦᐁᐊᐧᐠ.

ᑖᓂᓯ ᑫᖬ ᑳ ᐃᑎᑲᐃᐧᔭᐣ ᐃᓯ ᑲᑫᐧᒥᒣᐤ ᐊᐊᐧ ᐋᐸᑯᓴᐢ ᐆᐦᐅ ᐊᔭᐦᒋ ᐱᓯᐢᑭᐊᐧ. ᑯᐢᑯᒣᐤ ᐁᓴ ᒥᑐᓂ ᐁ ᑳᐧᐢᑯᐦᑎᖨᐟ.

ᐦᐅᐩ. ᑖᐯᐧ ᑭᑯᐢᑯᒥᐣ. ᓈᐯᐤ ᓀᖬ ᓂᑎᑎᑲᐃᐧᐣ ᐃᑌᐧᐤ ᐁᓴ ᐊᐊᐧ ᓀᔨᑳᒣᐢ ᑫᖬᐚᐤ ᒫᑲ.

ᐋᐸᑯᓴᐢ ᐆᒪ ᓀᖬ ᐃᑲᐧ ᐊᐊᐧ ᓂᑑᑌᒼ ᐚᐳᐢ ᐃᑖᐤ. ᑭᓄᐦᑌ ᐍᒣᐃᐧᓈᐣ ᓈ.

ᐦᐊᐤ ᐃᑌᐧᐤ ᐊᐊᐧ ᓈᐯᐤ. ᐃᑳᐧᓂ ᐊᑎ ᐅᑑᑌᒥᑐᐊᐧᐠ ᐃᑲᐧ ᐆᑯ ᓂᐢᑐ ᐱᓯᐢᑭᐊᐧᐠ.

ᐃᑳᐧᓂ ᑲᐧᔭᐢᐠ ᐃᑲᐧ ᒋᐦᑫᖨᐦᑕᒼ ᐊᐊᐧ ᐋᐸᑯᓴᐢ ᐊᖨᐢᐠ ᐁᑳ ᐊᐊᐧᓯᒣ ᐁ ᐱᖨᑯᐟ. ᐊᑎ ᒫᐦ ᒨᒋᑭᐦᑖᐊᐧᐠ ᐆᑯ ᓂᐢᑐ ᐱᓯᐢᑭᐊᐧᐠ.

ᑫᑕᐦᑕᐁᐧ ᐋᐸᑯᓴᐢ ᑳ ᐃᑌᖨᐦᑕᕽ ᓇᐊᐧᐨ ᒥᐢᑕᐦᐃ ᑭᑕ ᒨᒋᑭᐦᑖᐊᐧᐠ ᑫᐢᐱᐣ ᑯᑕᑲ ᐊᐃᐧᔭ ᑫ ᐊᑎ ᐅᑑᑌᒫᑖᐧᐃᐧ. ᑫ ᐊᑎ ᓯᐯᐧᐦᑌᐊᐧᐠ ᐃᑯᑕ ᐅᐦᒋ. ᑭᓀᐧᓴᐢ ᑫ ᐱᒧᐦᑌᐊᐧᐠ ᐆᑯ ᓂᐢᑐ ᐅᑑᑌᒫᑲᓇᐠ.

ᑫᑕᐦᑕᐁᐧ ᑳ ᐋᐧᐸᒫᒋᐠ ᐊᐃᐧᔭ ᐁ ᒪᑌᐧ ᓂᐹᔭᐟ ᐃᐢᐱᒥᕽ ᒥᐢᑎᑯᕽ ᐊᐧᑎᐦᑲᐧᓂᕽ ᒥᐢᑎᑯᕽ ᐁ ᓂᐹᔭᐟ ᐆᐦᐅ ᐱᓯᐢᑭᐊᐧ.

ᑖᐯᐧ ᒪᒪᐦᑖᐃᐧᓯᐤ ᓈᐦᐊ ᐱᓯᐢᑭᐤ ᐃᑌᐧᐤ ᐊᐊᐧ ᐋᐸᑯᓭᐢ. ᒫᐦᑎ ᐁᐧᓵᒫᑖᐣ ᑭᑕ ᐅᑑᑌᒥᑯᔭᕽ.

ᐃᑳᐧᓂ ᑌᐹᐧᑌᐊᐧᐠ ᑕ ᐯ ᓂᐦᑕᑯᓭᔭᐟ ᒥᐢᑎᑯᕽ ᐅᐦᒋ. ᓂᐦᒋ ᑳᐧᐢᑯᐦᑌᐤ ᐊᐊᐧ ᐊᔭᐦᒋ ᐱᓯᐢᑭᐤ ᐃᑯᑕ ᐅᐦᒋ.

ᐊᐧᐦᐋᐧ. ᐁ ᑫ ᐳᐋᐧᑕᑳᐧᐤ ᑯᑕᑲᐠ ᐱᓯᐢᑭᐊᐧᐠ ᐃᑌᐧᐤ ᐊᐊᐧ ᐊᔭᐦᒋ ᐱᓯᐢᑭᐤ ᐃᑲᐧ ᑖᐯᐧ ᑳ ᐯ ᑕᑯᓯᓂᔦᐠ.

ᑖᓂᓯ ᑫᔭ ᑭᑎᑎᑲᐃᐧᐣ ᐃᓯ ᑲᑫᐧᒋᒣᐤ ᐊᐊᐧ ᐋᐸᑯᓭᐢ ᐆᐦᐅ ᐊᔭᐦᒋ ᐱᓯᐢᑭᐊᐧ.

ᐴᓭᐢ ᐆᒪ ᓀᔭ ᐃᑌᐧᐤ ᐊᐊᐧ ᑫᔭᐋᐧᐤ ᒫᑲ.

ᐋᐸᑯᓭᐢ ᐆᒪ ᓀᔭ ᐃᑲᐧ ᐊᐊᐧ ᑭᓇᐦᒐᐋᐧᑳᐢ ᐋᐧᐳᐢ ᐃᑎᑲᐃᐧᐤ ᐃᑲᐧ ᐊᐊᐧ ᓄᓯᑳᒣᐢ ᓈᐯᐤ ᐃᑖᐤ. ᑭᓇᐦᑌ ᐁᐧᒣᐃᐧᓈᐣ ᓈ.

ᐦᐊᐤ ᑖᐯᐧ ᑕ ᑫ ᒨᒋᑲᐣ ᐃᑌᐧᐤ ᐊᐊᐧ ᐴᓭᐢ.

ᐃᑲᐧ ᒣᓇ ᐊᑎ ᓯᐯᐧᐦᑌᐊᐧᐠ ᐆᑯ ᐱᓭᐢᑭᐊᐧᐠ. ᐃᑳᐧᓂ ᓂᔦ ᐃᑲᐧ ᐱᓯᐢᑭᐊᐧᐠ ᐅᑑᑌᒥᑐᐊᐧᐠ. ᐸ ᐱᒧᐦᑌᐊᐧᐠ ᐃᑲᐧ ᒣᓇ ᐊᑎ ᒫᐦ ᒨᒋᑭᐦᑖᐊᐧᐠ.

ᐃᑲᐧ ᐋᑕ ᓵᓴᐩ ᓂᐢᑐ ᐁ ᐅᑑᑌᒥᐟ ᐊᐊᐧ ᐋᐸᑯᓭᐢ ᑭᔮᐱᐨ ᑯᑕᑲ ᓇᐦᑌ ᐅᑑᑌᒥᐤ ᓇᒨᔭ ᐅᐦᒋ ᓇᐦᐁᔭᐦᑕᑦ ᐊᐊᐧ ᐋᐸᑯᓭᐢ ᐋᑕ ᐃᔭᑯᕽ ᓵᓴᐩ ᓂᐢᑐ ᐱᓯᐢᑭᐊᐧ ᐁ ᐅᑑᑌᒥᐟ. ᑫᑕᐦᑕᐁᐧ

ᑳ ᓇᑭᐢᑲᐚᒋᐠ ᑯᑕᑲ ᐊᔭᐦᒋ ᐱᓯᐢᑭᐊᐧ. ᐊᐧᐃᐧᔭᓯᓇᐁᐧᐊᐧᐠ ᐆᐦᐅ ᐱᓯᐢᑭᐊᐧ ᐊᔭᐢᐠ ᐅᐯᐚᓴ ᓇᐊᐧᐨ ᐳᑯ ᐁ ᒋᒪᑌᔭᑭ.

ᐊᐧᐦᐋᐧ. ᐊᐁᐧᓇ ᐆᒪ ᑫᔭ ᐃᑌᐤ ᐁᓴ ᐊᐊᐧ ᐋᐸᑲᓴᐢ ᐆᐦᐅ ᐊᔭᐦᒋ ᐱᓯᐢᑭᐊᐧ.

ᑳᑲᐧ ᐆᒪ ᓀᔭ ᐃᑌᐧᐤ ᐊᐊᐧ ᐊᔭᐦᒋ ᐱᓯᐢᑭᐤ. ᑫᔭᐚᐤ ᒫᑲ ᐊᐁᐧᓂᑭ ᐆᒪ ᑫᔭᐚᐤ.

ᐋᐸᑯᓴᐢ ᐆᒪ ᓀᔭ ᐃᑌᐧᐤ ᐊᐊᐧ ᐋᐸᑯᓴᐢ. ᐃᑲᐧ ᐊᑎ ᐋᐩ ᐃᑕᐧᐦᐁᐤ ᐅᑑᑌᒪ ᑭᓯᐠ ᐁ ᐃᐧᐦᔮᐟ ᐚᐳᐢ ᐊᐊᐧ ᓈᐯᐤ ᐊᐊᐧ ᐃᑲᐧ ᐴᓴᐢ ᐊᐊᐧ. ᑭᓄᐦᑌ ᐅᑑᑌᒥᓈᐣ ᓈ.

ᐁᐦᐁ ᒪᐦᑎ ᒪᐦᑎ ᐃᑌᐧᐤ ᐊᐊᐧ ᑳᑲᐧ.

ᐃᑲᐧ ᒉᓇ ᐊᑎ ᓯᐯᐧᐦᑌᐊᐧᐠ ᐁ ᐊᑎ ᒫᐦ ᒉᑕᐁᐧᒋᐠ ᑲᐧᔭᐢᐠ ᒫᐦ ᒎᒋᑭᐦᑖᐊᐧᐠ. ᑫᑕᐦᑕᐁᐧ ᑯᑕᑲ ᐴᓴᓴ ᑳ ᓇᑭᐢᑲᐚᒋᐠ. ᐁᐧᒋ ᒉᑕᐁᐧᒉᐊᐧᐠ ᒉᓇ ᐃᔭᑯᓂ ᒫᑲ ᐯᔭᐢᐠ ᐊᑎ ᓀᐢᑐᓯᐊᐧᐠ ᐆᑯ ᐴᓴᓴᐠ.

ᑮᔮᑦ ᓇᑲᓯᓈᐣ ᐆᑕ ᐃᑌᐧᐤ ᐁᓴ ᐊᓇ ᐴᓴᐢ. ᒥᓴᐚᐨ ᓇᒎᔭ ᐊᐊᐧᓯᒉ ᓂᑲ ᐱᔭᑯᓈᐣ ᐊᔭᐢᐠ ᐁ ᒥᐢᑳᑐᔮᕽ.

ᐃᑳᐧᓂ ᐃᑯᑕ ᓇᑲᑌᐊᐧᐠ ᐊᓂᐦᐃ ᐴᓴᓴ. ᐯᑫᐧᔭᐦᑕᑦ ᐊᐊᐧ ᐋᐸᑯᓴᐢ ᐊᔭᐢᐠ ᐱᔭᐠ ᐅᑑᑌᒪ ᐁ ᐊᑎ ᓇᑲᑖᐟ. ᑫᑕᐦᑕᐁᐧ ᑯᑕᑲ ᑳᑲᐧ ᑳ ᓇᑭᐢᑲᐚᒋᐠ. ᓈᒋᐸᐦᐃᑐᐊᐧᐠ ᐆᑯ ᑳᑲᐧᐠ ᐃᑲᐧ ᐊᑎ ᓯᐯᐧᐸᐦᑖᐊᐧᐠ ᓵᑳᕽ. ᐦᐊᐩ. ᑲᐧᔭᐢᐠ ᐯᑫᐧᔭᐦᑕᒪᐧᐠ ᐆᑯ ᓂᐢᑐ ᐅᑑᑌᒫᑲᓇᐠ ᐊᔭᐢᐠ ᐁ ᐊᑎ ᐚᐦ ᐊᐧᓂᐦᐋᒋᐠ ᐅᑑᑌᒥᐚᐊᐧ.

ᑫᑕᐦᑕᐁᐧ ᑳ ᐊᑎ ᓄᐦᑌᑲᑌᐟ ᐊᐊᐧ ᓈᐯᐤ. ᐋᔮᔨᐦᑭᓀᐧ ᐅᐁᐧᒉᐚᐧᑲᓇ. ᑲᓇᐚᐧᐸᒣᐤ ᐋᐸᑯᓯᓴ. ᐋᑕᐁᐧᖨᒣᐤ ᐅᓯᑦ ᐁ ᐊᐱᓯᓯᓯᖨᐟ ᓇᒨᖬ ᑕ ᑫ ᑫᐢᐳᐤ ᒫᑲ ᐊᓂᐦᐃ ᐚᐧᐳᓴᐧ. ᐃᔭᑯᓂ ᐁᐧᖬ ᓇᐦᐁᖨᑯᕽ. ᑲᑫᐧ ᐅᑎᐦᑎᓀᐤ ᒫᑲ ᐚᐧᐳᐢ ᓯᐯᐧᐸᐦᑖᐤ ᓴᑳᕽ ᐁ ᐃᓯ ᑕᐸᓯᐟ. ᓇᐊᐧᓵᐧᑌᐤ ᐊᐊᐧ ᓈᐯᐤ ᐊᓂᐦᐃ ᐚᐧᐳᓴᐧ ᐁ ᐁᐧ ᒨᐚᐧᐟ.

ᑲᐧᔭᐢᐠ ᑭᓯᐚᐧᓯᐤ ᐊᐊᐧ ᐋᐸᑯᓯᐢ. ᐃᑳᐧᓂ ᑭᐦᒑᐧᑦ ᐁ ᐱᔭᑯᐟ. ᑲᐧᔭᐢᐠ ᑭᓯᐚᐧᐦᐃᐠ ᐊᓂᐦᐃ ᓈᐯᐊᐧ ᑳᐃᐧ ᓈᓂᑕᐤ ᐃᓯ ᐁᐧ ᐃᑑᑕᐁᐧᐤ ᐁᐧ ᐋᐯᐦᐅᐤ.

ᐁᔭᑯ ᐅᐦᒋ ᐊᓄᐦᐨ ᒫᓇ ᑳ ᑫᒧᒋ ᐁᐧᒫᔭᒫᐟ ᓈᐯᐊᐧ ᐊᐊᐧ ᐋᐸᑯᓯᐢ ᐁ ᒫᐦ ᒥᖪ ᑭᒧᑕᒪᐚᐧᐟ ᐅᒣᒋᐃᐧᓂᖨᐤ ᐊᓂᐦᐃ ᓈᐯᐊᐧ.

nīhithaw ācimowina

Woods Cree Stories

1.

wīsahkīcāhk ikwa okoskohowīsak

Wīsahkīcāhk and the Startlers

(1) wīsahkīcāhk ikwa okoskohowīsak

piyakwāw īsa wīsahkīcāhk kī-pa-pimohtīw. kītahtawī īsa wāpamīw pithīsisa.

"ho! nisīmitik!" itīw īsa. kanawāpamikow ōho pithīsisa. "nisīmitik, pithīsisak, tānisi kā-itikawiyīk?"

"sāsay kiwihthinān, 'pithīsisak,' kā-itwīyan ikosi kā-itikawiyāhk."

"nama! kahkithaw awiyak awasimīs wihthāw. tāpiskōc nītha: 'wīsahkīcāhk' nitisithihkāson māka 'ostīsimāw' mīna nititikawin. haw, tānisi kīthawāw kā-itikawiyīk?"

"namōtha nika-kī-wihtīnān. ninīkihikonānak ōko nikī-wihtamākonānak īkā ta-wihtamāhk kotak niwihthowininān 'okoskohowīsak' ī-itikawiyāhk."

"okoskohowīsak! ha!" kā-isi-pahpihāt īsa! "īsay, okoskohowīsak! nitakisiy, okoskohowīsak," itwīw īsa ī-ati-mīsātāt, ikwa anihi kā-patahwāt, otinīw ī-ati-kimisahwākīt!

"okoskohowīsak! osām kitapisīsisināwāw ta-koskohowīyīk," itwīw ī-ati-sipwīhtīt.

onīkihikomāwak koskwāpisinwak ispī kā-pī-kīwīcik.

"awīna awa kā-itōtahk! wahwā! kwayask kiwihcīkisināwāw! īsay!" itwīwak īsa.

(1) Wīsahkīcāhk and the Startlers

Once, Wīsahkīcāhk was walking about when all of a sudden, he saw some baby grouse.

"Ho! Honorable younger siblings!" says he to them. The baby grouse looked at him. "Honourable younger siblings, Baby Grouse, how are you called?"

"You already named us when you said 'Baby Grouse.' That's how we are called."

"No, everyone has more than one name. Like me: 'Wīsahkīcāhk' is my name but I am also called 'Oldest Brother.' Now, how are you called?"

"We can't tell. Our parents told us not to tell our other name 'Startlers' as we are called."

"Startlers! Ha!" He laughed at them. "Bosh, Startlers! My prick, Startlers," he said as he began to shit on them, and those he missed, he picked up and used them to wipe himself!

"Startlers! You are too small to scare me," he said beginning to leave.

The parents were so surprised when they got home.

"Who did this? Holy! You sure stink! Phew!" they said.

"wīsahkīcāhk ana," kā-isi-mātot īsa piyak pithīsis. "ī-pahkacimikoyāhk ta-wihtamāhk kotak kiwihthowininaw. mayaw 'okoskohowīsak' ī-itāyāhk kā-mīsātikoyāhk!"

"haw cīskwa wīsahkīcāhk!" itwīw awa nōsī-pithīw. nitomīw īsa kahkithaw otōtīma ta-māmawapicik. kī-nitawi-pīhowak pithīwak wāsakām sīpīhk ita māna wīsahkīcāhkwa kā-āsowakāmī-kwāskohtithit.

kītahtawī takohtīw awa nāpīw, kiyāpic ī-pahpihāt pithīsisa.

"okoskohowīsak! ha! īsay!" wāsakām sīpīhk takohtīw.

"ha! mahti nika-āsowakāmī-kwāskohtin!"

nīkān īsa asihtīw ikwa ikotī ohci pīcipahtāw. mwīhci sīpīhk ī-takopahtāt kā-nakīt.

"kīkāc," itwīw īsa; kā-wāpamāt piyak pithīsisa ī-ohpahothit sakāthihk ohci. kihtwām asihtīw ikwa mīna ati-sipwīpahtāw.

"kīkāc!" itwīw, ikwa mīna ī-nakīt. wāpamīw nīso pithīsisa ī-ohpahothit sakāthihk ohci. kihtwām asihtīw, nawac ikwa wahthawīs ohci ati-sipwīpahtāw.

"kīkāc!" itwīw, ī-nakīt ikwa mīna. nisto pithīsisa wāpamīw ī-ohpahothit sakāthihk ohci. kihtwām asihtīw, nawac wahthawīs ohci ati-sipwīpahtāw.

"It was Wīsahkīcāhk!" cried one baby grouse. "He tricked us to tell him our other name. As soon as we said 'Startlers', he shit on us!"

"Just you wait, Wīsahkīcāhk!" said the female grouse. She called all her tribesmen to have a meeting.

They went to wait along the river where Wīsahkīcāhk usually jumped across.

Eventually this man arrived, still laughing at the Startlers.

"Startlers! Ha! Bosh!"

He arrives along the river.

"Ha! Let's see, I'll jump across!"

First he backs up, then from there he runs and, just as he reaches the river, he stops.

"Almost!" he says. He sees a baby grouse fly up from the bushes. He backs up again, and again he begins to run.

"Almost!" he says, and once again he stops. He sees two baby grouse flying from the bush. He backs up again, and again he begins to run, this time from a little ways further.

"Almost!" he says, and once again, he stops. He sees three baby grouse flying from the bush.

mwīhci ī-ati-kwāskohtit kā-sasci-ohpahoyit mihcīt pithīwa! wahwā! kwayask, koskowithik! mitoni ī-ati-pakastawīsihk sīpīhk.

"okoskohowīsak, okoskohowīsak," kā-isi-pahpihikot īsa anihi okoskohowīsa!

ikwāni ī-iskwācimihcik okoskohowīsak.

He backs up again, this time he runs from further away. Just as he began his jump, lots of grouse flew out from the bushes. Wow! He was so startled that he landed in the water.

"okoskohowīsak! okoskohowīsak!" The grouse laughed at him saying their name.

That's the length of that story about the Startlers.

2.

wanisinwak nāpīsisak

Boys Get Lost

(2) wanisinwak nāpīsisak

kayās ōma kā-kī-awāsisīwiyān: mihcītwāw māna nikī-nitawīthihcikānān nīthanān, nistīs ikwa nisīmis. piyakwāw nikī-wanisininān! wahwā! kwayask nikī-wawānīthihtīnān athisk nikāwīnān ī-kī-itikoyāhk ta-pī-kīwīyāhk ati-tipiskāki.

"pī-kīwīhkīk ati-tipiskāki," kī-itwīw.

wahwā! tānisi māka ta-kī-isi-ati-kīwīyāhk ī-mwayī-tipiskāk! niwanohtānān sakāhk!

"āstam, pimitisahok," kā-itwīt nistīs. iyako ostīsimāw, mitātaht nīsosāp kī-itahtopiponīw. nipimitisahwānān. kinwīsk nipimitisahwānān māka āhci-poko niwanisininān. nawac mistahi nitati-wanisininān!

"awas! nītha ikwa nika-nīkānohtān," nititwān. "cikōci, wīpac kika-matāwisinaw!" nitisi-mamihcimon. mitātaht nītha nikī-itahtopiponān. kinwīsk nikī-pimohtānān māka āhci-poko sakāhk nitayānān. mitoni ati-otākosin, wīpac ta-pahkisimon! pīthisk nisīmis kā-ayamit.

"mahti nītha nika-nīkānohtān," itwīw nisīmis, wītha osīmimāw. nikanawāpamitonān nistīs ikwa nītha. nikī-ānwihtīnān ta-kaskihtāt ta-kīwīhtahikoyāhk athisk ayinānīw poko ī-kī-itahtopiponīt. kiyām nitati-pimitisahwānān. namōtha kinwīsk ispī kā-matāwisiyāhk ita kā-kī-kapīsiyāhk. mwīhci ī-ati-pahkisimok!

kiyāpic anohc wītha nisīmis nawac nihtā-nitawīthihcikīw. namōtha wihkāc wanisin.

(2) Boys Get Lost

Long ago when I was a child, we went grouse hunting a lot, me and my older brother and my younger brother. Once we got lost! Holy! We were at a loss as to what to do because our mother had told us to be home as night came on.

"Come before it starts to get dark!" she had said.

Holy! How are we to get home before it gets dark? We had lost our way in the bush.

"Come, follow me," said my older brother. He is the oldest; he was twelve years old at that time. We followed him. We followed him for a long time but we were still lost; in fact, we were more lost than before!

"Sheesh! My turn to lead the way," I said. "Watch, we will emerge from the bush in no time," I bragged. I was ten years old. We walked for a long time but we were still in the bush. It was getting to be late afternoon, early evening, soon it will begin to get dark. Eventually my younger brother spoke up.

"Let's see, I will lead the way," said my younger brother, he was the youngest. My older brother and I looked at each other. We doubted that he can successfully lead us home because he was only eight years old. No matter, we followed him. It didn't take long when we emerged from the bush, exactly where we had camped, just as the sun was setting!

Even to this day my younger brother is the best at hunting grouse. He never gets lost!

3.

kayās kā-makosī-kīsikāk

Long Ago Christmas

(3) kayās kā-makosī-kīsikāk

kayās māna, ispī kā-makosī-kīsikāk, mitoni māna wahthaw ohci kī-pā-pī-ohtohtīhowak athisitiniwak ta-pī-ayamihācik ōtī āmaciwīspimowinihk.

wahwā! kī-māh-mōcikihtākosiwak māna atimwak kā-pimitisahwastimwīhohcik athisk ī-kī-wawīsīhohcik. sīwīpicikanisa otāpāniyāpīwāhk ī-akotimimiht.

kihci-ayamihikimāw māna wīsta kī-pī-otāpahastimwīw! kwayask kī-māh-mithosiwak atimwak.

misiwīskamik māna kī-pā-pī-ohtohtīhowak athisitiniwak owahkōmākaniwāwa ī-pī-kāh-kiyokawācik ikwa mīna ī-āy-asotamākīcik ocawāsimisiwāwa ta-wīkihtothit ati-nīpinithiki.

kī-māh-mōcikan. kā-kīsi-ayamihāniwik kī-kāh-kiyokātowak athisitiniwak. kī-wāh-wihkōhkīwak ātiht, kahkithaw awiyak kī-māh-misi-mīcisow! ātiht mīna kī-māh-mīskoci-mīthitowak mīkiwina.

kwayask ikospī kī-āy-itahkamikan!

(3) Long Ago Christmas

Long ago, when it was Christmas, people would travel from far away to come for church services at Stanley Mission.

Holy! The dogs in their sled-teams made happy sounds because bells were attached to their harnesses.

Even the Bishop arrived by dog team! The dogs were very beautiful.

The people travelled from all over to come visit their relatives and betrothe their children for summer weddings.

It was lots of fun. When the church service was over the people visited one another. Some made feasts, everyone ate a lot … some exchanged gifts with one another.

Things were done properly back then.

4.

kohkominānihk

Grandmother's Bay

The following story is one told in and around Stanley Mission. I hope no one is offended by my writing it out for this collection.

(4) kohkominānihk

kayās īsa, mistahi māna kī-papāmohtīhowak ithiniwak, ī-nāh-nitonawācik pisiskiwa ta-pimātisihisocik. piyakwāw īsa ī-takwākinithik ōko ithiniwak āmaciwīspimowinihk ohci kī-sipwīhohtīhowak ikota ohci.

kī-ati-kapīsiwak nikiko-sākahikanihk, ikota piyak ī-misāthik wāsāw kā-kī-mānokīcik, piyak tipiskāw ikota kī-ayāwak. kā-kīkisīpāyāthik itasowīwak īsa ohcitaw poko ta-nakatācik piyak nōcokwīsiwa osām kīkāc ī-kawikihkāthit, ī-papīcīthit kā-mīkwā-pimohtīhocik.

ikota wāsāhk nakatamawīwak cīmānis ikwa kahkithaw otāpacihcikana. namōtha nānitaw ohci-itīthihtam awa nōcokwīsiw, ohcitaw māna ikosi ī-kī-itōtahkwāw kayās ithiniwak.

piyakwāw īsa ī-otākosinithik kā-wāpamāt mōswa awa nōcokwīsiw, ī-āsowahamithit sākahikan. hay! kīsiskaw pōsipathihow cīmānisihk, ī-tahkonahk pīminahkwān ikwa cīkahikanis, ī-nawaswātāt anihi mōswa. hay! kaskihtāw ta-tāpakwātāt, ikwa ikota ohci ati-cīkahwīw ostikwānithihk. kwayask nīpīhkwahisow!

kā-sīkwanithik īsa owahkōmākana kāwi takohtīhothiwa, ikota miskākow kiyāpic ī-ma-mīcithit kāskīwak, kapī-pipon īsa ī-māh-mōwāt anihi mōswa kā-kī-nipahāt.

ikospī ohci "kohkominānihk" pī-icikātīw iyako wāsāw ita kā-kī-piyako-piponisit awa nōcokwīsiw.

(4) Grandmother's Bay

A long time ago people would travel about in search of game that would keep them alive. One autumn these people from Stanley Mission travelled from there.

They camped along the way at Otter Lake, in one of the big bays in the area. They were there for one night. In the morning they decided that they would have to leave behind an old lady who was slowing them down because she was on the verge of keeling over from old age.

In that bay they left her with a small canoe and all her tools. The old lady thought nothing of this because that was the way things were done in those days.

One evening the old lady saw a moose swimming across the lake. Hey, quickly she jumped into the canoe. Taking with her a rope and a small axe, she chased the moose. Hey, she was able to snare the moose and then she hit the moose on the head. She had herself some game!

In the spring her relatives travelled back and there they found her still eating dry meat. Apparently she had eaten that moose she had killed all winter.

From that time on that bay where the old woman had spent the winter alone was known as Grandmother's Bay.

OUT OF
ORDER
HM 2013

5.

Shaking-Spear papāmohtīw

Shaking-Spear Wanders About

(5) *Shaking-Spear* papāmohtīw

piyakwāw īsa *Shaking-Spear* pa-pimohtīw mīskanāhk. wāpamīw mostoswa.

"tānisi," itwīw awa nāpīw.

"mōw, mōw," itwīw awa piyak mostos. koskohtawīw ōho mostoswa *Shaking-Spear*!

"hay! awas! namōtha ninohtī-mīcison," itwīw awa *Shaking-Spear*.

sāsay mīna pimohtīw mīskanāhk *Shaking-Spear*. wāpamīw māthacihkosa.

"tānisi," kā-itāt īsa ōho māthacihkosa.

"pā, pā," kā-itikot piyak māthacihkosa. wahwā! koskohtawīw!

"hay, awas! namōtha nītha kipāpā!" kā-itāt īsa.

ati-sipwīhtīw. kwayask kisiwāsiw!

(5) Shaking-Spear Wanders About

One time Shaking-Spear is walking along the road. He sees cows.

"Hello," he says to these cows.

"Moo, moo," says one cow. What the cow says surprises Shaking-Spear (for he heard the Cree word for "eat him, eat him").

"Hey! Go on! I don't want to eat," says Shaking-Spear.

Once again Shaking-Spear walks along the road. He sees sheep.

"Hello," he says to the sheep.

"Baa, baa," says this one sheep. Holy! What he hears surprises him (for he hears the Cree word for "father").

"Oh, go on! I am not your father," he says to him.

He begins to leave. He is very angry!

sāsay mīna pimohtīw mīskanāhk *Shaking-Spear.* ispatināhk wāpamīw mistikwa. mātow īsa awa mistik.

"tānīhki kā-mātoyan?" isi-kakwīcimīw ōho mistikwa.

"athisk tahto-kīsikāw awa piyak atim ī-sikisit," kā-isi-mātot awa mistik. kitimākihtawīw ōho mistikwa.

"haw, cīskwa kika-wīcihitin," itwīw īsa awa nāpīw. ati-masinahikīw.

ati-sipwīhtīw *Shaking-Spear.* cihkīthihtam athisk ī-wīcihāt mistikwa.

mwīscasīs īsa pī-takohtīw awa atim. wahwā! koskwāpisin! ayamihtāw anima kā-kī-masinahahk *Shaking-Spear*: *"Out of Order"* ī-itastīthik. ikwāni namōtha kaskihtāw ta-sikit. ati-sipwīhtīw. kisiwāsiw!

kwayask cihkīthihtam awa mistik.

Once again Shaking-Spear walks along the road. On top of a hill he sees a tree. This tree was crying.

"Why are you crying?" he asks this tree.

"Because every day this one dog comes and pees on me," cries the tree.

He takes pity on the tree.

"Okay, wait, I will help you," says this man. He begins to write.

Shaking-Spear begins to leave. He is happy because he had helped the tree.

A little while later the dog arrives. Holy, he is surprised at what he sees. He reads what Shaking-Spear had written. "Out of order" is what it read. Now he is unable to pee. He is angry!

The tree is very happy.

HM2013

6.

Shaking-Spear ikwa maskwa

Shaking-Spear and the Bear

(6) *Shaking-Spear* ikwa maskwa

piyakwāw ī-nīpinithik *Shaking-Spear* kī-nohtī-nitawiminīw. kī-pihtam ī-mihcītinithiki ithinimina anohc kā-nīpinithik. ikwāni kospiw. takahki-kīsikāthiw.

kinwīsīs nohcimihk sakāhk pa-pimohtīw ī-asawāpahtahk mīnisa. namōtha osām mistahi miskam. kā-kiskisit itī māna kā-kī-nitawiminīcik ispī kā-kī-awāsisīwit, namōtha osām wahthaw ita ohci kā-pimohtīt ... māka ohcitaw poko ta-āmaciwīt waciy.

ikwāni takohtīw ita ohci ta-ati-māci-āmaciwīt waciy. nisihkāc ati-ay-āmaciwīw, āskaw māna wāpahtam mīnisa, iyakoni ati-māh-mōminīw. pīthisk tahkohtāmatin takohtīw. ikota ohci asawāpiw. wahwā! mōcikāpisin! kwayask misiwīta ī-sīpihkwāthik, ithikohk ī-mīnisiskāthik. mōcikīthihtam! ikota sīmāk nahapipathihow, ī-ati-mawisot ikwa mīna āskaw ī-māh-mōminīsit.

mitoni kinwīsīs ma-mawisow, osām ī-otamīthot namwāc nākatawīthihtam ōma ita kā-ayāt. kītahtawī kā-pihtawāt awiya ī-pimahkamikisithit kihciwāk ita awa kā-mawisot. kīsiskaw asawāpiw. wahwā! wāpamīw maskwa ī-matwī-mōminīthit. kīsiskaw kāsōpathihow awa nāpīw. kostīw ōho maskwa. nisihkāc ati-sipwīhtīw ikota ohci. wahwā! wāpamikow ōho maskwa!

(6) Shaking-Spear and the Bear

One summer Shaking-Spear wanted to go berry-picking. He had heard that blueberries were numerous this summer. He went into the bush. It was a wonderful day.

He walked for a while deep in the bush looking for berries. He didn't find many. Then he remembered where they had gone berry-picking when he was a child. It wasn't far from where he was walking ... but he would have to climb a hill.

Eventually he arrived at the area from which he must climb the hill. He carefully climbed up. Sometimes he would see berries, and these he took to eat. Eventually he arrived on top of the hill. He looked about from there. Holy! His eyes beheld a wondrous sight! Everywhere there was blue, because berries were so numerous! He was happy. He plopped himself down right away, picking berries, and sometimes he would eat some of them.

He was picking berries for some time not paying attention to things around him. Suddenly he heard someone moving about nearby where he was picking berries. He quickly looked about. Holy! He sees a bear eating berries a little ways off. This man quickly hid, being scared of the bear. He carefully began to leave from there. Holy! The bear sees him!

kwahcipahtāw ikota ohci awa nāpīw, ī-nakacipahtāt omawisowin. wīsta maskwa kwahcipahtāw, ī-ati-nawaswātāt ōho nāpīwa. kwayask sīkisiw awa nāpīw!

ikwāni ati-nihtaciwīpahtāw awa nāpīw. wīsta maskwa ati-kakwī-nihtaciwīpahtāw. hay! ati-tāh-tīpwīw *Shaking-Spear* ithikohk ī-sīkisit. pihtawīw ōho maskwa, tāpiskōc wīpac ī-wī-otihtihikot. hay! kwayask kisīwīw awa maskwa, tāpiskōc ī-māh-matwīsihk sakāhk, nawac kihciwāk ī-pī-pihtākosithit. kītahtawī kā-wāpamāt *Shaking-Spear* ōho maskwa ī-miyāskākot! ī-pī-nihtaciwī-tihtipīpathithit īsa.

kipihcīw *Shaking-Spear* ī-ati-osāmi-pahpihāt anihi maskwa.

The man jumped from where he was running. The bear, too, jumped from where he was running, chasing this man. The man was very scared!

The man started running down the hill. The bear, too, started running down the hill. Hey! Shaking-Spear started yelling because he was so scared. He hears this bear, it was as if it would be soon overtake him. Hay! The bear was very loud, making sounds as if it was bouncing off the bushes, and the sounds sounded like they were much closer. All of a sudden, Shaking-Spear sees the bear go past him, rolling head over heels down hill.

Shaking-Spear had to stop because he was laughing so hard at the bear.

7.

paskwāwi-mostos mitahtahkwana

Buffalo Wings

(7) paskwāwi-mostos mitahtahkwana

kayās kimosōmipaninawak kī-nihtā-mācīwak. cīst, niwī-ācimāwak ōko. wihkāc nā kimīcin anihi mīciwinisa *'Buffalo Wings'* kā-icikātīki? paskwāwi-mostos mitahtahkwana anihi, wihkasinwa māna iyakoni!

haw, ka-wihtamātin ... kayās māna ispī nīhithawak kā-kī-nōcihācik paskwāwi-mostoswa namōtha māna katāc kī-wī-nipahīwak, tīpithahk māna otahtahkwaniwāwa ī-kī-nātwātahtahkwanihwācik, ithikohk ī-kī-nahīcik! tāpwī! ī-kaskitahtahkwanihwācik māna poko ōho paskwāwi-mostoswa ... paskwāwi-mostos mitahtahkwana wīstawāw ī-kī-wihkistahkwāw.

kāyitwihk kī-nāh-nahīwak! namōtha mwāsi kī-nāh-nipahīwak anihi paskwāwi-mostoswa. pīthisk kī-ati-mihcītiwak ōko paskwāwi-mostoswak, pīthisk ati-nāh-nihtāwikiwak paskwāwi-moscosisisak īkā awasimī ī-otahtahkwanicik, *"evolution"* ohci, iyako ohci *"evolution"* kā-icikātīk. iyako ohci anohc īkā awasimī ī-otahtahkwanicik ōko paskwāwi-mostoswak ... tāpwī anima! kwayask kī-nāh-nahīwak kayās kimosōmipaninawak!

mitoni kī-ati-osāmiyatiwak ōtī paskwāhk ōko paskwāwi-mostoswak īkā awasimī ī-otahtahkwanicik iyako ohci ōma ispī kā-takohtīhocik akāmaskihk ohci athisitiniwak, ōko mōniyāwak, namwāc wīthawāw ohci wāpamīwak paskwāwi-mostoswa ī-otahtahkwanithit.

(7) Buffalo Wings

A long time ago our Grandfathers were skillful hunters. Listen, I will tell a story about them. Have you ever eaten that food known as 'Buffalo Wings'? Those **are** buffalo wings—they are tasty!

Okay, I will tell you ... long ago when the Cree people went hunting buffalo they would not kill them. They were satisfied with knocking off their wings, that's how skillful they were! True! All they would do would be to cut off the wings from the buffalo ... they, too, liked the taste of buffalo wings.

They were true to their mark. They rarely killed the buffalo. Eventually the buffalo became numerous, and eventually the buffalo started to be born without wings. It's because of "evolution" — yes, that thing known as "evolution" is the reason that today the buffalo are born without wings. It's true! Our Grandfathers were very skilled hunters!

Eventually the buffalo became very numerous over there in the Prairies, no longer having any wings. That is why when the people from across the ocean arrived, these Caucasians, they never did see buffalo with wings.

māmaskāc māka ōko, mamahtāwisiwak!
kiyāpic pāh-piminawasowak, mīna atāwākīwak, ōho
paskwāwi-mostos mitahtahkwana!

tāpwī wihkasinwa!

But it is a wonder, they are so inventive.
They can still cook, and sell, buffalo wings.

They are truly tasty!

8.

mohcohkāsowin

Foolishness

(8) mohcohkāsowin

piyakwāw ī-kī-mātināwi-kīsikāk nikī-nohtī-ispathin kihci-mōhkomānaskīhk athisk ī-kwīta-pihtwāyān. nikī-nitawīthimāwak sikarītisak kihci-mōhkomāninähk ohci athisk iyakonik nawac ī-takahkispakosicik ithikohk ōta ohci kitaskīnāhk, kānatāhk.

ikwāni, wīpac ī-kīkisīpāyāk nikī-sipwīpathin. nikī-piyakohkīn. nīkān pitamā nikī-pihcipimān ikwa mīna pihkatīwāpoy timīsihk nikī-atāwīstamāson. ikwāni nikī-sipwīkocinin.

ispī kā-takopathiyān tipahaskānihk māka mīna nikakwīcimikawin tānitī ī-wī-ispathiyān ikwa mīna kīspin kinwīsk ikotī ī-wī-pimahkamikisiyān. niwihtamawāwak tipahaskān-kitīthihtamāwasowak tīpithahk *Plentywood*ihk kā-wī-ispathiyān ikwa mīna kanakī piyak kīsikāw kā-wī-pimahkamikisiyān ikotī. nipakitinikwak ta-akāmi-tipahaskānisiyān.

namōtha kinwīsk ispī kā-takopathiyān *Plentywood*ihk. nikipihcipathin atāwikamikohk ikwa ikota nitatāwīstamāson piyakwāyihk sikarītisak ikwa mīna nitatāwīstamawāw nitōtīm sōmināpoy. kā-pōnahkamikisiyān atāwikamikohk ninitonīn nānitaw ita ta-mīcisoyān ... nisihkāc nipimakocinin ... kītahtawī kā-wāpahtamān *"Harvest Moon Casino"*. sīmāk ikota nikipihcān ī-wī-nitawi-kakwī-otahikīyān mistahi sōniyāw, namōtha āhpō nikī-ohci-mīcison.

(8) Foolishness

One Saturday I wanted to go to the United States because I was in need of smokes. I wanted cigarettes from the States because they taste better than those here in our land, Canada.

With that idea, I left early in the morning. I went on my own. First I gassed up and got myself some coffee from Timmy's. I then took off.

When I got to the border I was, as usual, asked where I was going and if I was going to be there for a long time. I told the border guards that I was going as far as Plentywood and that I would at the least be one day. They let me go across the border.

It wasn't long before I arrived at Plentywood. I stopped at a store and bought myself a carton of cigarettes and also bought my friend a bottle of wine. When I was done at the store I looked for a place to eat ... I drove slowly ... all of a sudden I saw "Harvest Moon Casino." Right away, I stopped there with the idea that I was going to win lots of money. I didn't even eat.

kinwīsk ikota pihcāyihk kasīnōhk nimāthīthihcikān, āskaw nitotahikān māka nawac mistahi sōniyāw niwanihāw ... pīthisk nitati-mīscahokawin. wahwā mistahi nipīkwīthihtīn ispī kāwi kā-pōsiyān nitotāpānāskohk. nikitāpahtīn ithikohk pimiy kā-ayāyān ... iyaw! akāwāc ītokī nika-takopathin nīkihk ... mithopathihikoyāni oti. nama kīkway nitosōniyāmin, athisk ī-kī-mīscahokawiyān ikwāni namōtha nikaskihtān ta-atāwīstamāsoyān pimiy. nisihkāc nitati-kīwīkocinin. namōtha kinwīsk kā-nakatamān tipahaskān ispī sāsay kā-isinākwahk ī-ati-mīscipimīyān.

nitati-māh-mawimosin.

"ispathihikoyāni ta-tīpipathihikoyān pimiy nīkihk isko nama wihkāc kihtwām nika-māthīthihtīn kasīnow." ikosi nitisi-mawimosin. kītahtawī kā-pistahwak sikāk ... wahwā kwayask wihcīkisiw nitotāpānāskom.

"māmaskāc!" nititwān ikwa nitati-ākathāsīmon, *"God, I needed gas but not that kind of gas!"*

māmaskāc māni-māka, nikī-ati-mithopathihikon ... kaciskaw nīkihk ī-takopathiyān ispī kā-mīscipimīpathiyān!

I was inside the casino for a long time. Sometimes I won but I lost a lot more money … eventually all my money was gone! Holy, I was feeling sad when I got back in my car. I looked at how much gas I had ... oops! Maybe I can just make it home … if things go good for me. I had no money because I had lost it all so I was unable to buy any gas. I drove home slowly. Not long after leaving the border it looked like I was almost out of gas.

I began to pray over and over.

"If it should happen that I have enough gas to get me home, I will never again play the casino," is how my prayer went. All of a sudden I hit a skunk! Holy, the car stank!

"Goodness!" I said, and spoke in English, "God, I needed gas, but not that kind of gas!"

Wonders never cease, things went well for me. I just barely got home when I finally ran out of gas!

HM'13

9.

pisiskiwak otōtīmitowak

Animals Become Friends

(9) pisiskiwak otōtīmitowak

kayās īsa kī-pa-piyakowak ōko pisiskiwak. kwayask īsa awa piyak āpakosīs kī-kitimākīthimisow.

"matwān cī nānitaw itī nitotōtīmin," itīthihtam īsa. "mahti niwī-nitawi-nitonawāwak," itwīw īsa. ikwāni ati-sipwīhtīw. kinwīsk pa-pimohtīw awa āpakosīs. kītahtawī īsa awiya nakiskawīw.

nawac poko wawiyasinawīw ōho ayahci-pisiskiwa athisk ī-kinohtawakīthit. pa-piyahtak ōko nīso pisiskiwak ka-kitāpamitowak, ī-wa-wāskātitātocik, māka pīthisk kisiwāk ati-nātitowak. kāh-kakwīcimitowak.

"awīna ōma kītha," itwīw awa āpakosīs.

"wāpos māna nititikawin," itwīw awa kinohcawakās, awa ayahci-pisiskiw. "kītha māka, awīna ōma kītha?"

"āpakosīs ōma nītha," itwīw awa āpakosīs. "kinohtī-otōtīmimin nā?"

"haw, tāpwī," itwīw awa wāpos ... wīsta athisk ī-kī-pa-piyakot, ikwa wīsta awiya ī-kī-nohtī-otōtīmit.

ikwāni, ati-otōtīmitowak. ati-pimohtīwak mīskanāhk. kītahtawī wāpamīwak awiya ī-pimohtīthit mīskanāhk, ī-nīkānīskākocik. sakāsihk kāsōpathihowak, ikota ohci ī-kanawāpamācik ōho

(9) Animals Become Friends

A long time ago the animals lived on their own. This one mouse felt very sorry for himself because of that.

"I wonder if I have a friend anywhere?" he thought.

"Let's see, I'm going to go look for them," he says. He begins to leave. He walks for a long time, this mouse. All of a sudden he meets someone.

The sight of this strange animal amuses him because he has long ears. The two animals warily look over each other as they circle each other, but eventually approach each other. They ask one another questions.

"Who are you?" asks Mouse.

"I am usually called Rabbit," says Little Long Ears, this strange animal. "How about you, who are you?"

"Mouse is who I am," says Mouse. "Do you want to be friends?"

"Okay, for sure," says Rabbit ... he, too, had been alone, and he, too, wanted to have a friend.

They become friends. They walk along a road. All of a sudden they see someone on the road, walking ahead of them. They hide quickly in a small bush from where they watch this strange creature. They wonder

ayahci-pisiskiwa. māmaskātīwak, ikwa ati-kitimākinawīwak athisk ī-nīsokātīthit poko, ikwa mīna kaciskaw ī-opīwāthit. sākiskwīwak ōko nīso pisiskiwak ī-ati-sohkitīhīcik ikwa ati-ayamihīwak.

"tānisi kītha kā-itikawiyan?" isi-kakwīcimīw awa āpakosīs ōho ayahci-pisiskiwa. koskomīw īsa, mitoni ī-kwāskohtithit.

"hay! tāpwī kikoskomin! nāpīw nītha nititikawin," itwīw īsa awa nīsokācīs, "kīthawāw māka?"

"āpakosīs ōma nītha ikwa awa nitōtīm, wāpos itāw. kinohtī-wīcīwinān nā?"

"haw," itwīw awa nāpīw. ikwāni ati-otōtīmitowak ikwa ōko nisto pisiskiwak.

ikwāni kwayask ikwa cihkīthihtam awa āpakosīs athisk ikā awasimī ī-piyakot. ati-māh-mōcikihtāwak ōko nisto pisiskiwak.

kītahtawī āpakosīs kā-itīthihtahk nawac mistahi kita-mōcikihtāwak kīspin kotaka awiya kī-ati-otōtīmātwāwi. kī-ati-sipwīhtīwak ikota ohci. kinwīsīs kī-pimohtīwak ōko nisto otōtīmākanak.

kītahtawī kā-wāpamācik awiya ī-matwī-nipāthit ispimihk mistikohk, watihkwanihk mistikohk ī-nipāthit ōho pisiskiwa.

"tāpwī mamahtāwisiw nāha pisiskiw," itwīw awa āpakosīs. "mahti wīsāmātan kita-otōtīmikoyahk."

about him at first but then begin to take pity on him because he only has two legs and has very little hair! The two animals emerge from their hiding place. As they become braver they speak to him.

"What are you called?" asks Mouse of this strange animal. He startles him, making him jump.

"Hey! You surprised me! Man is what I am called," says Little Two-legged. "How about you guys?"

"Mouse is who I am and my friend is called Rabbit. Do you want to come with us?"

"Okay," says Man. They befriend one another, these three animals.

Now Mouse is really happy because he is no longer alone. These three animals begin to have fun.

All of a sudden Mouse thinks they can have more fun if they had another friend. They leave from there on their journey. The three friends walk for a bit of time.

All of a sudden they see someone sleeping up a tree, on a branch of a tree was where this animal was sleeping.

"Truly that creature is skillful," says Mouse, "Let's invite him to be our friend."

ikwāni tīpwātīwak ta-pī-nihtakosīthit mistikohk ohci. nihci-kwāskohtiw awa ayahci-pisiskiw ikota ohci.

"wahwā! ī-kī-powātakwāw kotakak pisiskiwak," itwīw awa ayahci-pisiskiw. "ikwa tāpwī kā-pī-takosiniyīk"

"tānisi kītha kititikawin?" isi-kakwīcimīw awa āpakosīs ōho ayahci-pisiskiwa.

"pōsīs ōma nītha," itwīw awa, "kīthawāw māka?"

"āpakosīs ōma nītha, ikwa awa kinohcawakās 'wāpos' itikawiw, ikwa awa nīsokācīs 'nāpīw' itāw. kinohtī-wīcīwinān nā?"

"haw tāpwī, ta-kī-mōcikan!" itwīw awa pōsīs.

ikwa mīna ati-sipwīhtīwak ōko pisiskiwak. ikwāni niyo ikwa pisiskiwak otōtīmitowak. pa-pimohtīwak ikwa mīna ati-māh-mōcikihtāwak.

ikwa āta sāsay nisto ī-otōtīmit awa āpakosīs kiyāpic kotaka nohtī-otōtīmiw, namōtha ohci nahīthihtam awa āpakosīs āta ithikohk sāsay nisto pisiskiwa ī-otōtīmit. kītahtawī kā-nakiskawācik kotaka ayahci-pisiskiwa. wawiyasinawīwak ōho pisiskiwa athisk opīwāsa nawac poko ī-cimatīthiki!

"wahwā! awīna ōma kītha?" itīw īsa awa āpakosīs ōho ayahci-pisiskiwa.

They shout at the creature to climb off the tree. The strange animal jumps down from the tree.

"Holy! I was dreaming of other animals," says this strange animal. "And truly you arrive!"

"What is it you are called?" asks Mouse of this strange animal.

"Cat is who I am," this one says, "and y'all?"

"Mouse is who I am, Little Long Ears is called 'Rabbit' and Little Two-legged is called 'Man.' Do you want to accompany us?"

"Okay, for sure, it could be fun!" says Cat.

Once again they begin to leave, these animals. Now there are four of them who are friends with one another. They walk along and also have lots of fun!

Although Mouse already has three friends, he begins to think that it would be more fun if he had another friend. He is not content with the three friends he already has. All of a sudden they meet up with another strange animal.

They are amused by the sight of this animal because its fur is sort of standing straight up!

"Holy! Who are you?" says Mouse to the strange animal.

"kākwa ōma nītha," itwīw awa ayahci-pisiskiw. "kīthawāw māka, awīniki ōma kīthawāw?"

"āpakosīs ōma nītha," itwīw awa āpakosīs. ikwa ati-āy-itwahīw otōtīma, kisik ī-wihthāt, "wāpos awa, nāpīw awa, ikwa pōsīs awa. kinohtī-otōtīminān nā?"

"īhī, mahti-mahti," itwīw awa kākwa.

ikwa mīna ati-sipwīhtīwak, ī-ati-māh-mītawīcik, kwayask māh-mōcikihtāwak. kītahtawī kotaka pōsīsa kā-nakiskawācik. wīci-mītawīmīwak mīna iyakoni māka pīthisk ati-nīstosiwak ōko pōsīsak.

"kiyām nakasinān ōta," itwīw īsa ana pōsīs. "misawāc namōtha awasimī nika-piyakonān athisk ī-miskātoyāhk."

ikwāni ikota nakatīwak anihi pōsīsa. pīkwīthihtam awa āpakosīs athisk piyak otōtīma ī-ati-nakatāt. kītahtawī kotaka kākwa kā-nakiskawācik. nācipahitowak ōko kākwak ikwa ati-sipwīpahtāwak sakāhk. hay! kwayask pīkwīthihtamwak ōko nisto otōtīmākanak athisk ī-ati-wāh-wanihācik otōtīmiwāwa!

kītahtawī kā-ati-nohtīkatīt awa nāpīw. ayāyihkinwī owīcīwākana. kanawāpamīw āpakosīsa. ātawīthimīw, osām ī-apisīsisithit, namōtha ta-kī-kīspow, māka anihi wāposwa? iyakoni wītha nahīthikohk. kakwī-otihtinīw māka wāpos sipwīpahtāw, sakāhk ī-isi-tapasīt. nawaswātīw awa nāpīw anihi wāposwa, ī-wī-mōwāt!

"Porcupine is who I am," says this strange animal. "How about you guys, who are y'all?"

"Mouse is who I am," says Mouse and he points to his friends, naming them as he continues, "This is Rabbit, this is Man, and this is Cat. Do you want to be friends with us?"

"Yes, for sure, for sure," says Porcupine.

So once again they set out. Along the way they play and they have lots of fun. All of a sudden they meet another cat. They play with this one, too, but eventually the cats get tired.

"You may as well leave us here," says Cat. "In any case, we are no longer alone because we have found each other.

So it was that they left Cat there. Mouse is sad because he has left one of his friends. All of a sudden they meet another porcupine. The two porcupines run for each other and disappear into the bush. Hay! The three friends who are left are very sad because they have begun to lose their friends.

All of a sudden Man gets hungry. His companions better be wary of him! He sizes up Mouse but rejects him because he is too small, he could not satisfy his hunger. Rabbit on the other hand? That one would be just perfect! He tries to grab for Rabbit, but Rabbit runs away into the bush. He escapes! Man chases after Rabbit, intending to eat him.

kwayask kisiwāsiw awa āpakosīs! ikwāni kihtwām ī-piyakot. kwayask kisiwāhik anihi nāpīwa, kāwi nānitaw isi wī-itōtawīw, wī-āpīhow!

iyako ohci anohc māna kā-kīmōci-wīc-āyāmāt nāpīwa awa āpakosīs, ī-māh-mitho-kimotamawāt omīciwinithiw anihi nāpīwa.

Mouse is very angry. He is once again alone. Man has made him angry. He plans on getting even, plans on revenge!

That is why to this day he lives close to man in secret, and in secret he enjoys stealing Man's food from him!

Woods Cree-English Glossary

Stem-Class Codes

INM	Indeclinable Nominal
IPC	Indeclinable Particle
IPH	Indeclinable Particle Phrase
IPL	Indeclinable Locative Particle
IPN	Prenoun
IPT	Indeclinable Temporal Particle
IPV	Preverb
NA	Animate Noun
NDA	Dependent Animate Noun
NDI	Dependent Inanimate Noun
NI	Inanimate Noun
PR	Pronoun
PrA	Animate Pronoun
PrI	Inanimate Pronoun
VAI	Animate Intransitive Verb
VII	Inanimate Intransitive Verb
VTA	Transitive Animate Verb
VTI	Transitive Inanimate Verb

Additional Abbreviations

1	first person
1p	first person plural exclusive
1s	first person singular
2	second person
21	first person plural inclusive
2p	second person plural
2s	second person singular
3	third person

3p	third person plural
3s	third person singular
3'	third person obviative
0	inanimate third person
0p	inanimate third person plural
0s	inanimate third person singular
0'p	inanimate third person obviative plural
0's	inanimate third person obviative singular
X	unspecified actor
>	action directed from one person to another
Conj	conjunct verb
Dim	diminutive noun; diminutive verb
Imp	imperative verb
Indc	indicative verb
Loc	locative
Neg	negative
Poss	possessor
Rcpl	reciprocal
Rdpl	reduplicated
Rflx	reflexive
s.o.	someone; animate object or goal of VTA
s.t.	something; inanimate object or goal of VTI
Subj	subjunctive verb (future conditional)
Voc	vocative (address form)

For further information on the organization of this glossary, please see the Introduction to this volume. For further information on the grammatical structure of Woods Cree and other Cree dialects, please consult appropriate language teaching texts such as *Cree Language Structures: A Cree Approach* (Ahenakew 1987a), *Cree, Language of the Plains* (Okimāsis 2004), and *A Woods Cree Grammar and Workbook* (Ratt 2009).

–(c)awāsimis– NDA_1 child [e.g. 3pPoss: *ocawāsimisiwāwa* "their child(ren)"; cf. NA_1 *awāsis–*]

–īk– NDI_4 home [e.g. 1sPoss/Loc: *nīkihk* "at my home"]

–kāwiy– NDA_2 mother [e.g. 1pPoss(3s): *nikāwīnān* "our mother"]

–mosōm– NDA_1 grandfather [e.g. 21Poss(3p): *kimosōmipaninawak* "our late grandfathers"]

–mosōmipan– NDA_1 late grandfather, deceased grandfather [e.g. 21Poss(3p): *kimosōmipaninawak* "our late grandfathers"]

–nīkihikw– NDA_3 parent [e.g. 1pPoss(3p): *ninīkihikonānak* "our parents"]

–ohkom– NDA_1 grandmother [cf. Loc: *kohkominānihk* "at Grandmother's Bay"]

–pāpā– NDA father, dad

–sīm– NDA_1 younger sibling [e.g. Voc plural: *nisīmitik* "my honourable younger siblings"]

–sīmis– NDA_1 younger sibling [Dim; e.g. 1sPoss(3s): *nisīmis* "my younger sibling"]

–stikwān– NDI_1 on another's head [e.g. 3'Poss(0')/Loc: *ostikwānithihk* "on another's head"]

–stīs– NDA_1 older brother [e.g. 1sPoss(3s): *nistīs* "my older brother"]

–tahtahkwan– NDI_1 wing [e.g. XPoss(0s): *mitahtahkwan* "wing"; 3sPoss(0'p): *otahtahkwana* "his/her/its wings"; 3pPoss(0'p): *otahtahkwaniwāwa* "their wings"]

–takisiy– NDI_2 intestine; [slang:] penis [e.g. 1sPoss(0s): *nitakisiy* "my penis"]

–(t)otāpānāskom– NDA_1 car [e.g. 1sPoss(3s): *nitotāpānāskom* "my car"; cf. NA_3 *otāpānāskw–*]

–tōtīm– NDA_1 friend; kinsman [e.g. 1sPoss(3s): *nitōtīm* "my friend; my kinsman"; 3sPoss(3'): *otōtīma* "his/her friend(s)"]

–wahkōmākan– NDA_1 relative [e.g. 3sPoss(3'): *owahkōmākana* "his/her relative(s)"; *owahkōmākaniwāwa* "their relative(s)"]

–wīcīwākan– NDA_1 companion [e.g. 3sPoss(3'): *owīcīwākana* "his/her companion(s)"]

akāmaskihk IPL land across the ocean

akāmi- IPV cross, across [e.g. *ta-akāmi-tipahiskānisiyān* "for me to cross the border"]

akāmi-tipahaskānisi– VAI_1 go across the border [e.g. *ta-akāmi-tipahiskānisiyān* "for me to cross the border"]

akāwāc IPC barely

akāwāc ītokī IPH maybe barely

akot– VTA_4 hang s.o. [2s>3s-Imp: *akos* "hang him/her"]

ana PrA that [medial animate singular demonstrative pronoun]

anima PrI that [medial inanimate singular demonstrative pronoun]

anihi PrA that, those [medial animate obviative demonstrative pronoun]

anihi PrI those [medial inanimate plural demonstrative pronoun]

anohc IPT today

apisīsisi– VAI_1 be small [e.g. 2p-Indc: *kitapisīsisināwāw* "you are little"; 3'-Conj: *ī-apisīsisithit* "(as) someone is small"]

asawāpahta– VTI_1 look around for s.t. [e.g. 3s-Conj: *ī-asawāpahtahk* "(as) s/he looks around for it"]

asawāpi– VAI_1 look around

asihtī– VAI_1 walk backwards

askiy– NI_2 land [e.g. 21Poss/Loc: *kitaskīnāhk* "in our land"]

asotamākī– VAI_1 promise, make promises

atāwākī– VAI_1 sell (s.t.)

atāwikamikohk IPL at the store [cf. NI_3 *atāwikamikw-*]

atāwikamikw– NI_3 store [Loc: *atāwikamikohk* "at the store"]

atāwīstamaw– VTA_2 buy (it) for s.o.

atāwīstamāso– VAI_1 buy (it) for oneself

athisitiniw– NA_2 person

athisk IPC because

ati- IPV begin to; progressively, along the way [e.g. *ati-ayamihīwak* "they begin to talk to s.o."; *ati-cīkahwīw* "s/he begins to chop s.o."; *ati-kitimākinawīwak* "they begin to take pity on s.o."; *kā-ati-nohtīkatīt* "when s/he begins to get hungry"]

atimw– NA_3 dog [singular: *atim*; plural: *atimwak*]

awa PrA this [proximal animate singular demonstrative pronoun]

awas IPC go away!

awasimī IPC more, further

awasimīs IPC a little more

awāsis– NA_1 child [e.g. 3pPoss: *ocawāsimisiwāwa* "their child(ren)"; cf. NDA_1 *–(c)awāsimis–*]

awāsisīwi– VAI_1 be a child

awiya PrA someone [indefinite animate obviative pronoun]

awiyak PrA someone [indefinite animate proximate pronoun]

awīna PrA who [animate singular interrogative pronoun]

awīniki PrA who (pl) [animate plural interrogative pronoun]

ay- IPV continually, ongoing [e.g. *ati-ay-āmaciwīw* "s/he began climbing up the hill"]

ayahci- IPN strange

ayahci-pisiskiw– NA_2 strange animal

ayami– VAI_1 speak

ayamih– VTA_1 talk to s.o. [e.g. 3p>0'-Indc: *ati-ayamihīwak* "they start to speak to another"]

ayamihā– VAI_1 pray, attend church service

ayamihikimāw– NA_2 priest

ayamihtā– VTI_2 read s.t.

ayā– VAI_1 be there, be located there [e.g. 3p-Indc: *kī-ayāwak* "they were there"]

ayā– VTI_2 have s.t. [e.g. 1s-Conj: *kā-ayāyān* "that which I have"]

ayāyihkinwī IPC better be careful! [exclamative]

ayinānīw IPC eight

ācim– VTA_1 tell a story about s.o.

āhci-poko IPH still

ākathāsīmo– VAI_1 speak English

āmaciwī– VAI_1 climb a hill [e.g. 3s-Indc: *ati-ay-āmaciwīw* "s/he began climbing up the hill"]

āmaciwīspimowinihk IPL Stanley Mission, SK [Loc; also NI_1 *āmaciwīspimowin–*]

ānwihta– VTI_1 disbelieve s.t. [e.g. 1p-Indc: *nikī-ānwihtīnān* "we disbelieve it"]

āpacihcikan– NI_1 tool [e.g. 3sPoss(0'p): *otāpacihcikana* "his/her tools"]

āpakosīs– NA_1 mouse

āpīho– VAI_1 have revenge, take revenge [e.g. 3s-Indc: *wī-āpīhow* "s/he is going to have revenge"]

āskaw IPT sometimes

āsowaha– VTI_1 cross water; cross s.t. (as a body of water) [e.g. 3'-Conj: *ī-āsowahamithit* "(as) someone is crossing the water"]

āsowakāmī- IPV across [e.g. *kā-āsowakāmī-kwāskohtit* "when s/he jumps across"]

āsowakāmī-kwāskohti– VAI_1 jump across [e.g. 3s-Conj: *kā-āsowakāmī-kwāskohtit* "when s/he jumps across"]

āstam IPC come here

āta IPC although

ātawīthim– VTA_1 reject s.o.

ātiht IPC some

āy- IPV repeatedly, again and again, here and there [Rdpl; e.g. *ī-āy-asotamākīcik* "as they are making promises"; *ati-āy-itwahīw* "s/he pointed at each of them in turn"]

cihkīthihta– VTI_1 be happy; enjoy s.t.

cimatī– VII_1 stand on end, stand upright [e.g. 0'p-Conj: *ī-cimatīthiki* "(as) they stand on end"]

cīkahikanis– NI_1 small axe [Dim]

cīkahw– VTA_3 chop s.o.

cīmānis– NI_1 small canoe [Dim; e.g. Loc: *cīmānisihk* "in the small canoe"]

cīmānisihk IPL in the small canoe [Loc; cf. NI_1 *cīmānis–*]

cīskwa IPT wait

cīst IPC listen up!

ha! IPC ha! [laughter]

haw IPC okay [agreement]
hay IPC hey! well! [exclamation of surprise]
ho! IPC well, what have we here?

icikātī– VII$_1$ be called thus [e.g. 0s-Indc: ... *icikātīw* "it is called ..."]
ikosi IPC so, thus; in that way; there
ikospī IPT at that time
ikospī ohci IPH from then on, from that time
ikota IPL there, at that place
ikota ohci IPH from there
ikotī IPL over there
ikotī ohci IPH from over there
ikwa IPC and; then
ikwa ikota IPH and then there
ikwa mīna IPH and also
ikwāni IPC and that was that; then
isi- IPV thus, that way [e.g. *ī-isi-tapasīt* "(as) s/he flees that way"]
isinākwan– VII$_2$ appear so, appear thus [e.g. 0s-Conj: *kā-isinākwahk* "it appeared so"]
isithihkāso– VAI$_1$ be called; be named [e.g. 1s-Indc: ... *nitisithihkāson* "I am called/named ..."]
isko IPC up to, as far as
iskwācim– VTA$_1$ tell a story about s.o. up to that point, tell so much of a story about s.o. [e.g. X>3p-Conj: *ī-iskwācimihcik* "that is the length of the story about them; they are told about up to that point"]
ispathi– VAI$_1$ go there; move toward; operate
ispathih– VTA$_1$ make it happen for s.o. [inanimate actor form: *ispathihiko–*]
ispatinaw– NI$_2$ hill [e.g. Loc: *ispatināhk* "on the hill"]
ispatināhk IPL up on a hill [Loc; cf. NI$_2$ *ispatinaw–* "hill"]
ispimihk IPL up, above
ispī IPC when
it– VTA$_4$ say so to s.o.; call s.o. so [e.g. 1p>3s-Conj: *ī-itāyāhk* "(as) we say to him"; 3'>3s-Indc: *itikow* "someone tells him/

her"; X>1s-Indc: ... *nititikawin* "I am called ..."; X>1p-Conj: *ī-itikawiyāhk* "(as) that is said to us"; X-3s-Indc: ... *itāw* "s/he is called ..."]

ita IPL there, where

ita ohci IPH from there

itahkamikan– VII$_2$ happen thus

itahtopiponī– VAI$_1$ be so many years old, be so many winters old

itasowī– VAI$_1$ decide thus [e.g. 3p-Indc: *itasowīwak* "they decide thus"]

itastī– VII$_1$ be set thus, be set in such a way [e.g. 0's-Conj: *ī-itastīthik* "(as) it is set in that way"]

ithikohk IPC so much

ithinimin– NI$_1$ blueberry [plural: *ithinimina*]

ithiniw– NA$_2$ person [commonly plural: *ithiniwak* "people"]

itī IPL there, where

itīthihta– VTI$_1$ think so about s.t.; think so [e.g. 3s-Conj: *kā-itīthihtahk* "what s/he thinks of it"; 3s-Indc: *ohci-itīthihtam* "s/he thinks thus that"]

itōta– VTI$_1$ do s.t. thus, do so [e.g. 3s>0'-Conj: *kā-itōtahk* "that is what s/he does"; 3p>0-Conj: *ī-kī-itōtahkwāw* "(as) they did it"]

itōtaw– VTA$_2$ do thus to s.o. [e.g. 3s>3'-Indc: *wī-itōtawīw* "s/he is going to do something to someone"]

itwah– VTA$_1$ point at s.o.

itwī– VAI$_1$ say so [e.g. 3s-Indc: *itwīw* "she says"; 2s-Conj: *kā-itwīyan* "that which you say"]

iyako PrA that one; that's the one [animate singular resumptive pronoun]

iyako PrI that one; that's the one [inanimate singular resumptive pronoun]

iyako ohci IPH for that reason; it is from that

iyakoni PrA that one, those ones [animate obviative resumptive pronoun]

iyakoni PrI those ones [inanimate plural resumptive pronoun]

iyakonik PrA those ones [animate plural resumptive pronoun]
iyaw IPC oops! well!
ī- IPV [grammatical preverb; marker of changed conjunct; e.g. *ī-ati-sipwīhtīt* "(as) s/he begins to leave"]
īhī IPC yes
īkā IPC no, not [negator for conjunct verb forms]
īkā awasimī IPH no longer, no further
īsa IPC evidently
īsay IPC bosh!; phew! [expression of disgust]
ītokī IPC I guess, maybe

ka- IPV will [future tense; e.g. *ka-wihtamātin* "I will tell you"]
ka-kī- IPV can, have the ability to; could; should [e.g. *nika-kī-wihtīnān* "we can tell about something"; cf. *ta-kī-*]
kaciskaw IPC barely
kahkithaw IPC all; every
kahkithaw awiyak PrA every one
kakwī- IPV try to [e.g. *kakwī-otihtinīw* "s/he tries to grab s.o."]
kakwīcim- VTA_1 ask s.o., ask s.o. a question [e.g. 3s>3'-Indc: *isi-kakwīcimīw* "s/he asks someone thus"]
kakwīcimito- VAI_1 ask each other [Rcpl]
kanakī IPT for a short while
kanawāpam- VTA_1 look at s.o. [e.g. 2s>3p-Imp: *kanawāpamik* "look at them"; 3s>3'-Indc: *kanawāpamīw* "s/he looks at someone"]
kanawāpamito- VAI_1 look at each other [Rcpl; e.g. 2s-Imp: *kanawāpamitok* "look at each other!"]
kapī-pipon IPT all winter
kapīsi- VAI_1 camp; camp for the night [e.g. 3s-Indc: *kapīsiw* "s/he camps"; 3p-Indc: *kī-ati-kapīsiwak* "they camped along the way"]
kasīnow- NI_2 casino [English borrowing; e.g. Loc: *kasīnōhk* "at the casino"]
kasīnōhk IPL at the casino [English borrowing; cf. *kasīnow-*]

kaskihtā– VTI$_2$ be successful at s.t., be able to do s.t.; achieve s.t.

kaskitahtahkwanihw– VTA$_1$ cut s.o.'s wings off

katāc IPC necessary [often in negative phrase]

kawikihkā– VAI$_1$ lean over with age, be extremely old [e.g. 3'-Conj: *ī-kawikihkāthit* "s.o. (obv) is leaning over with age"]

kayās IPT a long time ago

kā- IPV [grammatical preverb] [marker of changed conjunct; past tense; relative clause marker; e.g. *kā-ati-nohtīkatīt* "when s/he begins to get hungry"; *kā-itikawiyīk* "that is what you are called"; *kā-kīmōci-wīc-āyāmāt* "who s/he lives with in secret"]

kāh- IPV repeatedly; again and again, here and there [Rdpl; e.g. *kī-kāh-kiyokātowak* "they would visit one another"]

kākw– NA$_{4w}$ porcupine [singular: *kākwa*; plural: *kākwak*]

kānatāhk INM Canada, in Canada [cf. *kānatā*]

kāskīwakw– NI$_3$ dried meat [singular: *kāskīwak*]

kāsōpathiho– VAI$_1$ quickly hide; throw one oneself into hiding [e.g. 3p-Indc: *kāsōpathihowak* "they quickly hide"]

kāwi IPC back to; return

kāyitwihk IPC extremely so

kihci- IPN great; big

kihci-ayamihikimāw– NA$_2$ bishop

kihci-mōhkomān– NA$_1$ American [literally: "great-knife"; Loc: *kihci-mōhkomāninähk*]

kihci-mōhkomānaskiy– NI$_2$ America; the United States [literally: "long-knife land"; Loc: *kihci-mōhkomānaskīhk*]

kihci-mōhkomānaskīhk IPL in the United States [Loc; cf. NI$_2$ *kihci-mōhkomānaskiy–*]

kihci-mōhkomāninähk INM among the Americans, in the United States [Loc; cf. NA$_1$ *kihci-mōhkomān–*]

kihciwāk IPL close by [cf. *kisiwāk*]

kihtwām IPT again

kimisahwākī– VAI$_1$ wipe oneself with something, wipe one's ass with something [e.g. 3s-Conj: *ī-ati-kimisahwākīt* "(as) s/he begins to wipe with (it)"]

kimosōmipaninawak NDA$_1$ our late grandfathers [21Poss(3p); cf. NDA$_1$ *–mosōm–*, NDA$_1$ *–mosōmipan–*]

kimotamaw– VTA$_2$ steal from s.o. [e.g. 3s>3'-Conj: *ī-māh-mitho-kimotamawāt* "(as) s/he likes to steal from someone"]

kinohcawakās– NA$_1$ little long-eared one [Dim]

kinohtawakī– VAI$_1$ have long ears

kinwīsīs IPT a little while

kinwīsk IPT a long time

kipāpā NDA your dad [cf. *–pāpā–*]

kipihcipathi– VAI$_1$ stop one's motion, come to a sudden stop

kipihcī– VAI$_1$ stop, stop one's motion, stop driving [e.g. 3s-Indc: *kipihcīw* "s/he stops"]

kisik IPC while, at the same time

kisiwāh– VTA$_1$ make s.o. angry, anger s.o. [e.g. 3'>3s-Indc: *kisiwāhik* "someone makes him/her angry"]

kisiwāk IPL close by [cf. *kihciwāk*]

kisiwāsi– VAI$_1$ be angry [e.g. 3s-Indc: *kisiwāsiw* "s/he is angry"]

kisīwī– VII$_1$ be loud [e.g. 0s-Indc: *kisīwīw* "it is loud"]

kiskisi– VAI$_1$ remember [e.g. 3s-Conj: *kā-kiskisit* "s/he remembered"]

kita- IPV will [future tense; e.g. *kita-mōcikihtāwak* "they will have fun"; cf. *ka-*]

kitaskīnāhk IPL in our land [21Poss/Loc; cf. NI$_2$ *askiy–*]

kitāpahta– VTI$_1$ look at s.t.

kitāpamito– VAI$_1$ look at each other [Rcpl; e.g. 3p-Indc: *kitāpamitowak* "they look at each other"]

kitimākihtaw– VTA$_2$ hear s.o. with pity, take pity on s.o. upon hearing that one [e.g. 3s>3'-Indc: *kitimākihtawīw* "s/he takes pity upon someone through hearing them"]

kitimākinaw– VTA$_2$ take pity on s.o.

kitimākīthimiso– VAI$_1$ have self pity, think oneself pitiful [Rflx]

kiyām IPC it doesn't matter; may as well

kiyāpic IPC still

kiyokaw– VTA$_2$ visit s.o.

kiyokāto– VAI$_1$ visit each other [Rcpl; e.g. 3p-Indc: *kī-kāh-kiyokātowak* "they would visit each other"]

kī- IPV [grammatical preverb: past tense] [e.g. *kī-ati-kapīsiwak* "they camped along the way"; *ī-kī-itōtahkwāw* "(as) they did this"; *kā-kī-mānokīcik* "when they set up camp"]

kīkāc IPC almost

kīkisīpāyā– VII$_1$ be morning [e.g. 0s-Indc: *kīkisīpāyāw* "it is morning"; 0's-Conj: *kā-kīkisīpāyāthik* "in the morning"]

kīmōci- IPV in secret [e.g. *kā-kīmōci-wīc-āyāmāt* "who s/he lives with in secret"]

kīsi– IPV finish

kīsiskaw IPC quickly

kīspin IPC if

kīspo– VAI$_1$ be full [e.g. 3s-Indc: *ta-kī-kīspow* "s/he could be full"]

kītahtawī IPT all of a sudden

kītha PrA you, yours [second person singular personal pronoun]

kīthawāw PrA you (pl), yours (pl) [second person plural personal pronoun]

kīwī– VAI$_1$ go home [e.g. 3p-Conj: *kā-pī-kīwīcik* "when they come home"]

kīwīhtah– VTA$_1$ take s.o. home [e.g. 3'>3s-Indc: *kīwīhtahikow* "someone takes him/her home"]

kīwīkocin– VAI$_2$ drive toward home

kohkominānihk INM Grandmother's Bay [literally: "place of the Grandmother"; cf. NDA$_1$ *–ohkom–*]

koskohowī– VAI$_1$ surprise people; startle people [e.g. 2p-Conj: *ta-koskohowīyīk* "for you (pl) to startle people"]

koskohtaw– VTA$_2$ be surprised upon hearing s.o. [e.g. 3s>3'-Indc: *koskohtawīw* "s/he is surprised upon hearing what someone says"]

koskom– VTA$_1$ startle s.o. verbally, surprise s.o. with words [e.g. 2s>1s-Indc: *kikoskomin* "you startled me with words"; 3s>3'-Indc: *koskomīw* "s/he startles someone with words"]

koskowith– VTA_1 surprise s.o.; startle s.o. [e.g. 3'>3s-Indc: *koskowithik* "someone surprises him/her"]

koskwāpisin– VAI_2 be surprised by a sight [e.g. 3p-Indc: *koskwāpisinwak* "they are surprised by a sight"]

kospi– VAI_1 go into the bush

kost– VTA_4 be scared of s.o., be frightened of s.o. [e.g. 3s>3'-Indc: *kostīw* "s/he is scared of someone"]

kotak PR another [animate and inanimate singular indefinite pronoun]

kotaka PrA another, others [animate obviative indefinite pronoun]

kotakak PrA others [animate plural indefinite pronoun]

kwahcipahtā– VAI_1 jump up running

kwayask IPC right; properly; extremely

kwāskohti– VAI_1 jump [e.g. 1s-Indc: *nika-āsowakāmī-kwāskohtin* "I will jump across"; 3s-Conj: *ī-ati-kwāskohtit* "(as) s/he begins to jump"; 3'-Conj: *ī-kwāskohtithit* "(as) another jumped"; 3s-Conj: *kā-āsowakāmī-kwāskohtit* "when s/he jumps across"]

kwīta- IPV be short of, be in need of

kwīta-pihtwā– VAI_1 be in need of smokes; be short of tobacco

ma- IPV continuously, ongoing [reduplication; *ī-ma-mīcithit* "(as) another is eating"; *ma-mawisow* "s/he is gathering berries"]

mahti IPC please; let's [e.g. *mahti wīsāmātan* "let's invite him/her"]

mahti-mahti IPC let's see, let's see

makosī-kīsikā– VII_1 be Christmas Day [e.g. 0s-Conj: *kā-makosī-kīsikāk* "when it was Christmas Day"]

mamahtāwisi– VAI_1 be skillful, be gifted with skills [e.g. 3s-Indc: *mamahtāwisiw* "he/she is skillful"]

mamihcimo– VAI_1 brag; boast [e.g. 3s-Indc: *mamihcimow* "s/he brags"]

masinaha– VTI_1 write s.t. [e.g. 3s-Conj: *kā-kī-masinahahk* "that which he had written"]

masinahikī– VAI$_1$ write [e.g. 3s-Indc: *ati-masinahikīw* "s/he began writing"]

maskw– NA$_{4w}$ bear [singular: *maskwa*]

matāwisi– VAI$_1$ emerge from the bush [e.g. 3s-Indp: *matāwisiw* "s/he emerges from the bush"]

matwān cī IPH maybe, I wonder

matwī- IPV visible in the distance, audible at a distance [e.g. *ī-matwī-nipāthit* "(as) another sleeps in the distance; (as) s/he snores"]

matwīsin– VAI$_2$ make a sound by falling, make a sound from bouncing on something [e.g. 3s-Conj: *ī-māh-matwīsihk* "(as) s/he makes a sound from bouncing on something"]

mawimosi– VAI$_1$ pray, pray a little [Dim; e.g. Rdpl/1s-Indc: *nimāh-mawimosin* "I pray repeatedly; I keep saying little prayers"]

mawiso– VAI$_1$ pick berries to eat right away [e.g. 3s-Indc: *ma-mawisow* "s/he is gathering berries"]

mawisowin– NI$_1$ harvest of berries; the gathering of berries [e.g. 3sPoss(0's): *omawisowin* "his/her harvest of berries"]

mayaw IPT as soon as

māci- IPV start, begin to [e.g. *ta-ati-māci-āmaciwīt* "for him/her to start going uphill"]

mācī– VAI$_1$ hunt, hunt big game

māh- IPV repeatedly; again and again, here and there [Rdpl; e.g. *ī-māh-matwīsihk* "(as) s/he makes a sound from bouncing on something"; *ī-māh-mōwāt* "(as) s/he eats something again and again"; *ī-māh-mitho-kimotamawāt* "(as) s/he likes to steal from someone"; *kī-māh-mōcikihtākosiwak* "they made joyful sounds; they were heard pleasurably"; *ī-ati-māh-mītawīcik* "they are repeatedly playing along the way"]

māka IPC but

māka mīna IPH as usual

māmaskāc IPC it is a wonder; amazing

māmaskāt– VTA$_4$ wonder about s.o. [e.g. 3p>3'-Indc: *māmaskātīwak* "they wonder about someone"]

māmawapi– VAI$_1$ meet, have a meeting [e.g. 3p-Conj: *ta-māmawapicik* "for them to meet"]
māna IPC usually
māni-māka IPC for sure
mānokī– VAI$_1$ set up camp, set up tents [e.g. 3p-Conj: *kā-kī-mānokīcik* "when they set up camp"]
māthacihkos– NA$_1$ sheep; lamb [Dim]
māthīthihcikī– VAI$_1$ have a challenging attitude; be disrespectful
māthīthihta– VTI$_1$ challenge s.t.; think ill of s.t.
mātināwi-kīsikā– VII$_1$ be Saturday [e.g. 0s-Conj: *ī-kī-mātināwi-kīsikāk* "(as) it was Saturday"]
māto– VAI$_1$ cry [e.g. 3s-Conj: *kā-isi-mātot* "how s/he cries"]
mihcīt IPT lots; many
mihcīti– VAI$_1$ be plentiful, be numerous
mihcītin– VII$_2$ be many, be numerous [e.g. 0p-Indc: *mihcītinwa* "there are many of them"]
mihcītwāw IPT lots of times; many times
misawāc IPC in any case
misā– VII$_1$ be big [e.g. 0's-Conj: *ī-misāthik* "(as) it is big"]
misi– IPV big; much, a lot [e.g. *kī-māh-misi-mīcisow* "s/he would eat and eat and eat"]
misiwīskamik IPL everywhere, all over the world
misiwīta IPL everywhere
miska– VTI$_1$ find s.t.
miskaw– VTA$_2$ find s.o. [e.g. 3'>3s-Indc: *miskākow* "someone finds him/her"]
miskāto– VAI$_1$ find each other [Rcpl; e.g. 21-Conj: *ī-miskātoyahk* "(as) we found each other"]
mistahi IPC lots, much; a great amount
mistikohk IPL in the tree [Loc; cf. NA$_3$ *mistikw–*]
mistikw– NA$_3$ tree [singular: *mistik*]
mitahtahkwan NDI$_1$ wing [cf. *–tahtahkwan–*]
mitātaht IPC ten
mitātaht nīsosāp IPC twelve

mitho- IPV good, well [e.g. *ī-māh-mitho-kimotamawāt* "(as) s/he likes to steal from someone"]

mithopathih- VTA$_1$ make good things happen for s.o., cause s.o. to have good fortune [e.g. 0>1s-Subj: *mithopathihikoyāni* "if things go well for me"]

mithosi- VAI$_1$ be attractive, be good-looking [e.g. 3p-Indc: *kī-māh-mithosiwak* "they were always good-looking"]

mitoni IPC very

miyāskaw- VTA$_2$ pass s.o., go past s.o. [e.g. 3'>3s-Conj: *ī-miyāskākot* "(as) someone goes past him"]

mīci- VTI$_3$ eat s.t. [e.g. 3'-Conj: *ī-ma-mīcithit* "(as) another is eating"]

mīciso- VAI$_1$ eat

mīciwin- NI$_1$ food [e.g. 3'Poss(0's): *omīciwinithiw* "someone's food"]

mīciwinis- NI$_1$ food, small bit of food [Dim; e.g. plural: *mīciwinisa* "bits of food"]

mīkiwin- NI$_1$ gift

mīkwā- IPV while; simultaneously [e.g. *kā-mīkwā-pimohtīhocik* "while they travel"]

mīna IPC and, also

mīnis- NI$_1$ berry [plural: *mīnisa*]

mīnisiskā- VII$_1$ be an abundance of berries; berries are numerous [e.g. 0s-Indc: *mīnisiskāw* "berries are numerous"]

mīsāt- VTA$_4$ defecate on s.o.; shit on s.o. [e.g. 3s>3'-Conj: *ī-ati-mīsātāt* "(as) s/he defecates on someone"; 3s>1p-Conj: *kā-mīsātikoyāhk* "s/he who defecates on us"]

mīscahw- VTA$_3$ use up all s.o. or s.o.'s possessions [e.g. X>1s-Indc: *nitati-mīscahokawin* "it was all used up on me"; X>1s-Conj: *ī-kī-mīscahokawiyān* "I had lost it all"]

mīscipimī- VAI$_1$ run out of gas, use up all one's gasoline [e.g. 1p-Conj: *ī-ati-mīscipimīyān* "that I was starting to run out of gas"]

mīscipimīpathi- VAI$_1$ run out of gas suddenly

mīskanaw- NI$_2$ road [e.g. Loc *mīskanāhk* "road"]

mīskanāhk IPL on the road [Loc; cf. NI_2 *mīskanaw–* "road"]
mīskoci– IPV in turn, in exchange [e.g. *kī-māh-mīskoci-mīthitowak* "they would exchange gifts with one another"]
mītawī– VAI_1 play [e.g. 3p-Conj: *ī-ati-māh-mītawīcik* "they are playing along the way"]
mīthito– VAI_1 exchange gifts; give gifts to one another [e.g. 3p-Indc: *kī-māh-mīskoci-mīthitowak* "they would exchange gifts with one another"]
mohcohkāsowin– NI_1 foolishness
mostosw– NA_3 cow [singular: *mostos*]
mōcikan– VII_2 be fun [e.g. 0s-Indc: *ta-kī-mōcikan* "it could be fun"]
mōcikāpisin– VAI_2 enjoy the sight of something
mōcikihtā– VTI_2 have fun (with s.t.) [e.g. 3p-Indc: *ati-māh-mōcikihtāwak* "they have fun along the way"; 3p-Indc: *kita-mōcikihtāwak* "they will have fun"]
mōcikihtākosi– VAI_1 sound exciting, sound pleasurable; make a sound which brings joy [e.g. 3p-Indc: *kī-māh-mōcikihtākosiwak* "they made joyful sounds; they were heard pleasurably"]
mōcikīthihta– VTI_1 be happy about s.t.; find s.t. fun; have a good time
mōminī– VAI_1 eat berries [e.g. Rdpl/3s-Indc: *ati-māh-mōminīw* "s/he begins eating berries"]
mōminīsi– VAI_1 eat berries a bit [Dim; e.g. Rdpl/3s-Conj: *ī-māh-mōminīsit* "(as) s/he keeps nibbling at the berries"]
mōniyāw– NA_2 caucasian, white-man
mōsw– NA_{4w} moose [singular: *mōswa*]
mōw– VTA_1 eat s.o. [e.g. 3s>3'-Conj: *ī-māh-mōwāt* "(as) s/he eats s.o. continuously"; 3s>3'-Conj: *ī-wī-mōwāt* "(as) s/he is going to eat someone"]
mwayī- IPV before
mwāsi IPC [see *namōtha mwāsi*]
mwīhci IPC exactly; at that exact time
mwīscasīs IPT a little while later

nahapipathiho– VAI$_1$ sit right down
nahī– VAI$_1$ be right on the mark, be skilled
nahīthihta– VTI$_1$ be satisfied (with s.t.) [e.g. 3p>0-Indc: nahīthihtam "s/he is satisfied"]
nahīthikohk IPC enough
nakacipahtā– VAI$_1$ run, leaving something behind
nakat– VTA$_4$ leave s.o. behind [e.g. 3p>3'-Indc: *nakatīwak* "they leave someone"; 3s>3'-Conj: *ī-ati-nakatāt* "s/he leaves someone behind along the way"; 3p>3'-Conj: *ta-nakatācik* "for them to leave someone"; 2s>1p-Imp: *nakasinān* "leave us behind!"]
nakata– VTI$_1$ leave s.t.
nakatamaw– VTA$_2$ leave (it) for s.o. [e.g. 3p>3'-Indc: *nakatamawīwak* "they leave it for someone"]
nakiskaw– VTA$_2$ meet s.o. [e.g. 3p>3'-Conj: *kā-nakiskawācik* "when they meet someone"]
nakī– VAI$_1$ stop [e.g. 3s-Conj: *ī-nakīt* "(as) s/he stops"; 3s-Conj: *kā-nakīt* "when s/he stops"]
nama IPC no
nama kīkway IPH nothing
nama wihkāc IPH never
namōtha IPC no; not
namōtha āhpō IPH not even
namōtha awasimī IPH no longer
namōtha katāc IPH not necessary
namōtha kinwīsk IPH not long
namōtha mwāsi IPH rarely
namōtha osām IPH not that much
namōtha wihkāc IPH never
namwāc IPC no
nawac IPC better; more than
nawac mistahi IPH more so
nawac poko IPH more likely; more or less, sort of, rather
nawaswāt– VTA$_4$ chase s.o., pursue s.o.; follow s.o. [e.g. 3s-3'-Indc: *nawaswātīw* "s/he chases someone"; 3s>3'-Conj:

ī-nawaswātāt "(as) s/he chases someone; (as) s/he follows someone"]

nā IPC [question particle] [e.g. *kinohtī-otōtīminān nā?* "do you want to be friends with us?"]

nācipahito– VAI$_1$ run toward each other [Rcpl; e.g. 3p-Indc: *nācipahitowak* "they run toward each other"]

nāh- IPV repeatedly, here and there, again and again [Rdpl; e.g. *ī-nāh-nitonawācik* "(as) they look for another"]

nāha PrA that one over there [distal animate singular demonstrative pronoun]

nākatawīthihta– VTI$_1$ be wary of s.t.; take care

nānitaw IPC around, about; in some way

nānitaw isi IPH in some way, in any way

nānitaw ita IPH somewhere

nānitaw itī IPH somewhere

nāpīsis– NA$_1$ boy [Dim; plural: *nāpīsisak*]

nāpīw– NA$_2$ man

nātito– VAI$_1$ approach each other [Rcpl; e.g. 3p-Indc: *nātitowak* "they approach each other"]

nātwātahtahkwanihw– VTA$_1$ knock the wings off s.o.

nihci- IPV down, downwards

nihci-kwāskohti– VAI$_1$ jump down

nihtaciwī– VAI$_1$ go downhill [e.g. 3'-Conj: *ī-pī-nihtaciwī-tihtipīpathithit* "(as) s/he came rolling down the hill"]

nihtaciwīpahtā– VAI$_1$ run downhill

nihtakosī– VAI$_1$ climb down [e.g. 3'-Conj: *ta-pī-nihtakosīthit* "for someone to come climbing down"]

nihtā– IPV be skilled at, be good at, be known for [e.g. *kī-nihtā-mācīwak* "they were good hunters"; *nihtā-nitawīthihcikīw* "s/he is good at hunting grouse"]

nihtāwiki– VAI$_1$ be born [e.g. 3p-Indc: *ati-nāh-nihtāwikiwak* "they are starting to be born"]

nikāwīnān NDA$_2$ our mother [1pPoss(3s); cf. *–kāwiy–* "mother"]

nikiko- IPN pertaining to an otter [e.g. *nikiko-sākahikanihk* "at Otter Lake"]

nikiko-sākahikan– NI_1 Otter Lake [e.g. Loc: *nikiko-sākahikanihk* "at Otter Lake"; cf. *nikikw–* "otter"]
nikikw– NA_3 otter [e.g. *nikiko-sākahikanihk* "at Otter Lake"]
ninīkihikonānak NDA_3 our parents [1pPoss(3p); cf. *–nīkihikw–* "parent"]
nipah– VTA_1 kill s.o. [e.g. 3s>3'-Conj: *kā-kī-nipahāt* "when s/he killed someone"]
nipā– VAI_1 sleep [e.g. 3'-Conj: *ī-matwī-nipāthit* "(as) another sleeps in the distance; (as) s/he snores"]
nisihkāc IPC carefully, slowly
nisīmis NDA_1 my younger sibling [1sPoss(3s); cf. *–sīmis–*]
nisīmitik NDA_1 my honorable younger siblings [Voc plural; cf. *–sīm–*]
nistīs NDA_1 my older brother [1sPoss(3s); cf. *–stīs–*]
nisto IPC three
nitakisiy NDI_2 my intestine; [slang:] my penis [1sPoss(0s); cf. *–takisiy–*]
nitawi- IPV go to [e.g. *kī-nitawi-pīhowak* "they went to wait"]
nitawiminī– VAI_1 go search for berries
nitawīthihcikī– VAI_1 want things; go grouse-hunting [e.g. 1p-Indc: *nikī-nitawīthihcikānān* "we went grouse-hunting"]
nitawīthim– VTA_1 want s.o.
nitom– VTA_1 invite s.o.
nitona– VTI_1 look for s.t.
nitonaw– VTA_2 look for s.o. [e.g. 3p>3'-Conj: *ī-nāh-nitonawācik* "(as) they look for someone"]
nitotāpānāskom NDA_1 my car [e.g. 1sPoss(3s): *nitotāpānāskom* "my car"; cf. *–(t)otāpanāskom–*; NA_3 *otāpānāskw–*]
nitōtīm NDA_1 my friend; my kinsman [1sPoss(3s); cf. *–tōtīm–*]
niyo IPC four
nīhithaw– NA_2 Cree person [e.g. plural: *nīhithawak* "Cree people"]
nīkān IPC first

nīkānīskaw– VTA$_2$ be in front of s.o. [e.g. 3'>3p-Conj: *ī-nīkānīskākocik* "(as) someone is in front of them"]

nīkānohtī– VAI$_1$ lead, walk in the lead

nīkihk IPL at my home [1sPoss/Loc; cf. NDI$_4$ *–īk–*]

nīpīhkwahiso– VAI$_1$ kill game for oneself [Rflx; e.g. 3s-Indc: *nīpīhkwahisow* "s/he kills game for him/herself"]

nīpin– VII$_2$ be summer

nīso IPC two

nīsokācīs– NA$_1$ little two-legged one; human being [Dim]

nīsokātī– VAI$_1$ have two legs, be two-legged [e.g. 3'-Conj: *ī-nīsokātīthit* "(as) another has two legs"]

nīstosi– VAI$_1$ be tired [e.g. 3p-Indc: *ati-nīstosiwak* "they start to tire"]

nītha PrA I, me, mine [first person singular personal pronoun]

nīthanān PrA we, us, ours [first person plural exclusive personal pronoun; "we but not you"]

nohcimihk IPL inland; in the bush

nohtī- IPV want to [e.g. *kinohtī-otōtīminān nā?* "do you want to be friends with us?"; *ī-kī-nohtī-otōtīmit* "(as) s/he wanted to have friends"]

nohtīkatī– VAI$_1$ be hungry [e.g. 3s-Conj: *kā-ati-nohtīkatīt* "when s/he begins to get hungry"]

nōcih– VTA$_1$ hunt s.o. with skill; mean on s.o.

nōcokwīsiw– NA$_2$ old lady, old woman

nōkwan– VII$_2$ appear, be visible

nōsī-pithīw– NA$_2$ female grouse

ohci IPC from

ohci- IPV from there

ohci-itīthihta– VTI$_1$ think thus from that [e.g. 3s-Indc: *ohci-itīthihtam* "s/he thinks thus that"]

ohcitaw IPC it has to be; necessarily; obligatorily

ohpaho– VAI$_1$ fly up, fly into the air [e.g. 3p-Conj: *kā-sasci-ohpahocik* "when they suddenly fly up"; 3'-Conj: *ī-ohpahothit* "(as) another flew up"]

ohtohtīho– VAI$_1$ travel from there
okoskohowīs– NA$_1$ Startler; one who startles others [Dim]
onīkihikomāw– NA$_2$ parent [e.g. plural: *onīkihikomāwak* "parents"]
opīwā– VAI$_1$ have fur; have hair; have plumage [e.g. 3'-Conj: *ī-opīwāthit* "(as) another has fur, hair"]
opīwāsa NA$_1$ his/her fur [3sPoss; cf. *pīwās*–]
osām IPC because; too
osāmi- IPV too much, overly [e.g. *ī-ati-osāmi-pahpihāt* "s/he is laughing at him/her too much"]
osāmiyati– VAI$_1$ be many, be in excessive numbers [e.g. 3s-Indc: *osāmiyatiw* "s/he is many"]
osīmimāw– NA$_2$ youngest sibling [cf. NDA$_1$ –*sīm*–]
osōniyāmi– VAI$_1$ have money [e.g. 1s-Indc: *nitosōniyāmin* "I have money"]
ostikwān NDI$_1$ his/her head [3sPoss(0's); e.g. 3'Poss(0')/Loc: *ostikwānithihk*; cf. –*stikwān*–]
ostīsimāw– NA$_2$ eldest brother [cf. NDA$_1$ –*stīs*– "elder brother"]
otahikī– VAI$_1$ win at a challenge
otahtahkwaniwāwa NDI$_1$ their wings [3pPoss(0'p); cf. –*tahtahkwan*– "wing"]
otahtahkwani– VAI$_1$ have wings
otamītho– VAI$_1$ be busy, be occupied by something
otākosin– VII$_2$ be evening [e.g. 0's-Conj: *ī-otākosinithik* "(as) it is evening"]
otāpahastimwī– VAI$_1$ drive a dog-team
otāpānāskw– NA$_3$ car [e.g. 1sPoss(3s): *nitotāpānāskom* "my car"]
otāpāniyāpiy– NI$_2$ harness
oti IPC ! [emphatic particle; follows emphasised word]
otihtih– VTA$_1$ reach s.o.; overtake s.o. [e.g. 3'>3s-Conj: *ī-wī-otihtihikot* "(as) someone is going to reach him/her"]
otihtin– VTA$_1$ grab s.o. [e.g. 3s>3'-Indc: *kakwī-otihtinīw* "s/he tries to grab s.o."]
otin– VTA$_1$ take s.o.

otōtīm(im)- VTA$_1$ befriend s.o. [e.g. 2s>1p-Indc: *kinohtī-otōtīminān nā?* "do you want to be friends with us?"; 3p>3'-Subj: *kī-ati-otōtīmātwāwi* "when/if they befriended someone"; 2s>1s-Imp: *otōtīmimin* "be friends with me!"]

otōtīma NDA$_1$ his/her friend(s) [3sPoss(3'); cf. *-tōtīm-*]

otōtīmākan- NA$_1$ friend [e.g. plural: *otōtīmākanak* "friends"; cf. NDA$_1$ *-tōtīm-*]

otōtīmi- VAI$_1$ have (s.o. as a) friend [e.g. 1s-Indc: *nitotōtīmin* "I have friends"; 3s-Conj: *ī-kī-nohtī-otōtīmit* "(as) s/he wanted to have friends"]

otōtīmito- VAI$_1$ be friends, befriend one another [Rcpl; e.g. 2p-Imp: *otōtīmitok* "be friends with each other!"]

owahkōmākana NDA$_1$ his/her relative(s) [3sPoss(3'); cf. *-wahkōmākan-*]

owīcīwākana NDA$_1$ his/her companion(s) [3sPoss(3'); cf. *-wīcīwākan-*]

ōho PrA that, these [proximal animate obviative demonstrative pronoun]

ōko PrA these [proximal animate plural demonstrative pronoun]

ōma IPC it is [emphatic focus particle]

ōma PrI this [proximal/obviative inanimate singular demonstrative pronoun]

ōta IPL here

ōta ohci IPH from here

ōtī IPL over here

pa- IPV continuously [Rdpl; e.g. *pa-pimohtīw* "s/he walks about"]

pa-piyahtak IPC careful, carefully [Rdpl]

pahkacim- VTA$_1$ fool s.o. verbally, fool s.o. with words [e.g. 3s>1p-Conj: *ī-pahkacimikoyāhk* "(as) s/he fooled us with words"]

pahkisimon- VII$_2$ the sun sets

pahpih- VTA$_1$ laughs at s.o. [e.g. 3s>3'-Conj: *ī-pahpihāt* "(as) s/he laughed at somone"; 3s>3'-Conj: *ī-ati-osāmi-pahpihāt* "(as) s/he is laughing at someone too much"; 3'>3s-Conj: *kā-isi-pahpihikot* "how someone laughs at him/her"]

pakastawīsin– VAI$_2$ fall in the water [e.g. 3s-Conj: *ī-pakastawīsihk* "(as) s/he falls in the water"]

pakitin– VTA$_1$ allow s.o.; let s.o.

papāmohtī– VAI$_1$ wander about

papāmohtīho– VAI$_1$ travel about [e.g. 3p-Indc: *kī-papāmohtīhowak* "they travelled about"]

papīcī– VAI$_1$ be slow [e.g. 3'-Conj: *ī-papīcīthit* "(as) another is slow"]

paskwāhk IPL on the prairies [Loc; cf. NI$_2$ *paskwāw*–]

paskwāw– NI$_2$ plains, prairies [e.g. Loc: *paskwāhk* "on the prairies"]

paskwāwi-moscosisis– NA$_1$ buffalo calf [Dim]

paskwāwi-mostosw– NA$_3$ buffalo [singular: *paskwāwi-mostos*]

patahw– VTA$_3$ miss s.o. (by shot) [e.g. 3s>3'-Conj: *kā-patahwāt* "when s/he misses someone"]

pā– IPV around, about [e.g. *kī-pā-pī-ohtohtīhowak* "they came travelling from all over"; also: *papā-*]

pihcāyihk IPL inside

pihcipimī– VAI$_1$ gas up, put gasoline in the tank

pihkatīwāpoy– NI$_2$ coffee

pihta– VTI$_1$ hear s.t. [e.g. 3s>0'-Indc: *pihtam* "s/he hears it"]

pihtaw– VTA$_2$ hear s.o. [e.g. 3s>3'-Conj: *kā-pihtawāt* "another whom s/he heard"]

pihtākosi– VAI$_1$ make a sound; be heard [e.g. 3'-Conj: *ī-pī-pihtākosithit* "(as) another is heard approaching"]

pihtwā– VAI$_1$ smoke; have a smoke

pimahkamikisi– VAI$_1$ move about doing something

pimakocin– VAI$_2$ move along, drive along

pimātisihiso– VAI$_1$ make a living for oneself [Rflx; e.g. 3p-Conj: *ta-pimātisihisocik* "for them to make a living for themselves"]

piminawaso– VAI$_1$ cook, prepare a meal

pimitisahw– VTA$_3$ follow s.o.

pimitisahwastimwīhw– VTA_3 make s.o. follow (as a dog team) [e.g. X>3p-Conj: *kā-pimitisahwastimwīhohcik* "those who were made to follow as a dog-team"]

pimiy– NI_2 gas; oil; grease

pimohtī– VAI_1 walk, walk about [e.g. Rdpl/3s-Indc: *pa-pimohtīw* "s/he walks about"]

pimohtīho– VAI_1 travel, travel along [e.g. 3p-Conj: *kā-mīkwā-pimohtīhocik* "while they travel"]

piponisi– VAI_1 spend the winter, pass the winter [e.g. 3s-Conj: *kā-kī-piyako-piponisit* "when s/he wintered alone"]

pisiskiw– NA_2 animal

pistahw– VTA_3 hit s.o. accidentally

pitamā IPT for now

pithīsis– NA_1 little grouse [Dim; e.g. plural: *pithīsisak* "little grouse"]

pithīw– NA_2 grouse [plural: *pithīwak*]

piyahtak IPC careful, carefully

piyak IPC one

piyak kīsikāw IPT one day

piyak tipiskāw IPT one night

piyako- IPV alone; by oneself [e.g. *kā-kī-piyako-piponisit* "when s/he wintered alone"]

piyako– VAI_1 be alone [e.g. 1p-Indc: *nika-piyakonān* "we will be alone"]

piyakohka– VTI_1 be in a vehicle alone; tend to s.t. alone [e.g. 1s>0-Indc: nikī-piyakohkīn "I was alone in the vehicle"]

piyakwāw IPC once

piyakwāyihk IPC one set, one unit; one carton

pī- IPV come, come to [e.g. *ī-pī-nihtaciwī-tihtipīpathithit* "(as) s/he comes rolling down the hill"]

pī-icikātī– VII_1 come to be called thus [e.g. 0s-Indc: *pī-icikātīw* "it comes to be called thus"]

pīcipahtā– VAI_1 come running; run towards speaker [e.g. 3s-Indc: *pīcipahtāw* "s/ he runs over this way"]

pīho– VAI_1 wait [e.g. 3p-Indc: *kī-nitawi-pīhowak* "they went to wait"]

pīkwīthihta– VTI$_1$ be sad; be sad over s.t.

pīminahkwān– NI$_1$ rope

pīthisk IPC finally; eventually

pīwās– NI$_1$ little fur, hair, pelt, plumage [Dim; e.g. 3sPoss(0'p): *opīwāsa* "his/her little hair/fur"]

poko IPC only, just

powāt– VTA$_4$ dream about s.o. [e.g. 1s>3p-Conj: *ī-kī-powātakwāw* "(as) I dreamed about them"]

pōnahkamikisi– VAI$_1$ stop one's activity, stop doing something

pōsi– VAI$_1$ get on board; board a vehicle

pōsipathiho– VAI$_1$ board quickly, jump aboard

pōsīs– NA$_1$ cat [Dim]

sakāhk IPL in the bush [Loc; cf. NI$_2$ *sakāw*–]

sakās– NI$_1$ brush; small area of bush [Dim; e.g. Loc: *sakāsihk* "in the brush"]

sakāsihk IPL in the brush, in the bush [Loc; cf. NI$_1$ *sakās*–]

sakāw– NI$_2$ bush, woods [e.g. Loc: *sakāhk* "in the bush"]

sasci- IPV suddenly [e.g. *kā-sasci-ohpahoyit* "when they suddenly fly up"]

sākahikan– NI$_1$ lake [e.g. Loc: *nikiko-sākahikanihk* "at Otter Lake"; cf. nikikw– "otter"]

sākiskwī– VAI$_1$ emerge; stick out one's head [e.g. 3p-Indc: *sākiskwīwak* "they emerge"]

sāsay IPT already

sikarītis– NA$_1$ cigarette [English borrowing; Dim; commonly plural: *sikarītisak* "cigarettes"]

sikākw– NA$_3$ skunk [singular: *sikāk* "skunk"]

siki– VAI$_1$ pee, urinate [e.g. 3s-Conj: *ta-sikit* " for him/her to pee"]

sikit– VTA$_4$ pee on s.o., urinate on s.o. [e.g. 3s>1s-Conj: *ī-sikisit* "(as) s/he pees on me"]

sipwīhohtīho– VAI$_1$ leave on one's travels, set off to travel [e.g. 3p-Indc: *kī-sipwīhohtīhowak* "they left on their travels"]

sipwīhtī– VAI$_1$ leave, depart [e.g. 3s-Conj: *ī-ati-sipwīhtīt* "(as) s/he begins to leave"]
sipwīkocin– VAI$_2$ speed away, go away fast, go forward fast
sipwīpahtā– VAI$_1$ run away, leave at a run
sipwīpathi– VAI$_1$ drive away; go forward, go away
sīkisi– VAI$_1$ be afraid
sīkwan– VII$_2$ be spring [e.g. 0's-Conj: *kā-sīkwanithik* "in the spring"]
sīmāk IPT right away, immediately
sīpihkwā– VII$_1$ be blue [e.g. 0's-Conj: *ī-sīpihkwāthik* "(as) another is blue"]
sīpiy– NI$_2$ river [e.g. Loc: *sīpīhk* "in/on/at the river"]
sīpīhk IPL in/on/at the river [Loc; cf. NI$_2$ *sīpiy–* "river"]
sīwīpicikanis– NA$_1$ bell [Dim]
sohkitīhī– VAI$_1$ be brave; have a strong heart [e.g. 3s-Conj: *ī-ati-sohkitīhīcik* "(as) they begin to be brave"]
sōmināpoy– NI$_2$ wine
sōniyāw– NA$_2$ money

ta- IPV [grammatical preverb, marker of the conjunct; irrealis; infinitival 'to'] [e.g. *ta-koskohowīyīk* "for you (pl) to startle people"; *ta-māmawapicik* "for them to meet"; cf. *ka-*]
ta-kī- IPV can; could; should [e.g. *ta-kī-kīspow* "s/he could be full"; *ta-kī-mōcikan* "it could be fun"; cf. *ka-kī-*]
tahkohtāmatin IPL on top of a hill
tahkona– VTI$_1$ carry s.t., takes s.t. along [e.g. 3s>0-Conj: *ī-tahkonahk* "(as) s/he carries it"]
tahto-kīsikāw IPT every day
takahki-kīsikā– VII$_1$ be a great day [e.g. 0s-Indc: *takahki-kīsikāw* "it is a great day"]
takahkispakosi– VAI$_1$ taste good
takohtī– VAI$_1$ arrive by foot
takohtīho– VAI$_1$ arrive from travelling [e.g. 3'-Indc: *kāwi takohtīhothiwa* "someone comes travelling back"]
takopahtā– VAI$_1$ arrive running [e.g. 3s-Conj: *ī-takopahtāt* "(as) s/he arrives running"]

takopathi– VAI$_1$ arrive by vehicle
takosin– VAI$_2$ arrive [e.g. 2p-Conj: *kā-pī-takosiniyīk* "when you(pl) arrive"]
takwākin– VII$_2$ be autumn, be fall [e.g. 0's-Conj: *ī-takwākinithik* "(as) it is autumn"]
tapasī– VAI$_1$ flee [e.g. 3s-Conj: *ī-isi-tapasīt* "(as) s/he flees that way"]
tāh- IPV repeatedly, again and again [e.g. *ati-tāh-tīpwīw* "s/he begins shouting"]
tānisi IPC how; hello, how are you
tānitī IPL where
tānīhki IPC why
tāpakwāt– VTA$_4$ snare s.o. [e.g. 3s>3'-Conj: *ta-tāpakwātāt* "for him/her to snare someone"]
tāpiskōc IPC as if, just like; it seems
tāpwī IPC true, truly; really
tihtipīpathi– VAI$_1$ roll [e.g. 3'-Conj: *ī-pī-nihtaciwī-tihtipīpathithit* "(as) s/he came rolling down the hill"]
timīsihk INM at Timmy's, at Tim Horton's [Loc; English borrowing: *timīs–* "Timmies / Timmy's'"]
tipahaskān– NI$_1$ border [e.g. Loc: *tipahaskānihk* "at the border"]
tipahaskān-kitīthihtamāwasow– NA$_2$ border guard [plural: *tipahaskān-kitīthihtamāwasowak*]
tipahaskānihk IPL at the border [Loc; cf. NI$_1$ *tipahaskān–*]
tipiskā– VII$_1$ be night [e.g. 0s-Indc: *tipiskāw* "it is night"]
tipiskāw IPT night, time period of one night's duration
tīpipathih– VTA$_1$ make s.o. last [e.g. inanimate actor form *tīpipathihiko–*]
tīpithahk IPC at least; just barely
tīpwāt– VTA$_4$ call s.o. [e.g. 3p>3'-Conj: *tīpwātīwak* "they call someone"]
tīpwī– VAI$_1$ shout [e.g. *ati-tāh-tīpwīw* "s/he begins to shout"]

wa- IPV continuously, ongoing [reduplication; *ī-wa-wāskātitātocik* "(as) they are circling each other"]

waciy– NI_2 hill, range of hills
wahthaw IPL far away
wahthawīs IPL a little ways
wahwā! IPC oh my! [an exclamative]
wanih– VTA_1 lose s.o. [e.g. 1s>3s-Indc: *niwanihāw* "I lose him/her"; 3p>3'-Conj: *ī-ati-wāh-wanihācik* "(as) they begin losing others"]
wanisin– VAI_2 be lost
wanohtī– VAI_1 lose one's way
watihkwan– NI_1 branch [e.g. Loc: *watihkwanihk*]
watihkwanihk IPL on the branch [Loc; cf. NI_1 *watihkwan–*]
wawānīthihta– VTI_1 be confused (by s.t.)
wawiyasinaw– VTA_2 find s.o.'s looks comical
wawīsīhw– VTA_3 dress s.o. up, decorate s.o. [e.g. X>3p-Conj: *ī-kī-wawīsīhohcik* "(as) they were decorated"]
wāh- IPV repeatedly, again and again [Rdpl; e.g. *ī-ati-wāh-wanihācik* "(as) they begin losing others"]
wāpahta– VTI_1 see s.t.
wāpam– VTA_1 see s.o. [e.g. 3p>3'-Conj: *kā-wāpamācik* "when they see someone"; 3'>3s-Indc: *wāpamikow* "someone sees him/her; s/he is seen by someone"]
wāposw– NA_3 rabbit [singular: *wāpos*]
wāsakām IPL around, along
wāsāhk IPL in the bay [Loc; cf. NI_2 *wāsāw–*]
wāsāw– NI_2 bay [e.g. Loc: *wāsāhk* "in the bay"]
wāskātitāto– VAI_1 circle each other [Rcpl: e.g. 3p-Conj: *ī-wa-wāskātitātocik* "(as) they circle each other"]
wihcīkisi– VAI_1 stink, smell very badly [e.g. 2p-Indc: *kiwihcīkisināwāw* "you (pl) stink"]
wihkasin– VII_2 be tasty, be delicious [e.g. 0p-Indc: *wihkasinwa* "they are tasty"]
wihkāc IPT ever
wihkista– VTI_1 like the taste of s.t.
wihkōhkī– VAI_1 have a feast

wihta– VTI$_1$ tell about s.t. [e.g. 1p>0s-Indc: *nika-kī-wihtīnān* "we can tell about something"; 1p>0s-Conj: *ta-wihtamāhk* "for us to tell it"]

wihtamaw– VTA$_2$ tell (it to) s.o. [e.g. 1s>2s-Indp: *ka-wihtamātin* "I will tell you"; 3p>1p-Indc: *nīkī-wihtamākonānak* "they told us"]

wihth– VTA$_1$ name s.o. [e.g. 2s>1p-Indc: *kiwihthinān* "you name us"; X>3s-Indc: *wihthāw* "he/she is named"]

wihthowin– NI$_1$ name [e.g. 1pPoss(0s): *niwihthowininān* "our name"; 21Poss(0s): *kiwihthowininaw* "our name"]

wī– IPV going to, intend to [prospective aspect; e.g. *ī-wī-mōwāt* "(as) s/he is going to eat someone"; *ī-wī-otihtihikot* "(as) someone is going to reach him/her"; *wī-āpīhow* "s/he is going to have revenge"]

wīc-āyām– VTA$_1$ live with s.o. [e.g. 3s>3'-Conj: *kā-kīmōci-wīc-āyāmāt* "who s/he lives with in secret"]

wīci-mītawīm– VTA$_1$ play with s.o. [e.g. 3p>3'-Indc: *wīci-mītawīmīwak* "they play with someone"]

wīcih– VTA$_1$ help s.o. [e.g. 1s>2s-Indc: *kika-wīcihitin* "I will help you"]

wīcīw– VTA$_2$ accompany s.o. [e.g. 2s>1p-Indc: *kinohtī-wīcīwinān* "you want to accompany us"]

wīkihto– VAI$_1$ be married; marry one another

wīpac IPT soon; early

wīsahkīcāhkw– NA$_3$ Wīsahkīcāhk

wīsām– VTA$_1$ invite s.o. [e.g. 21>3s-Imp: *mahti wīsāmātan* "let's invite him/her"]

wīsta PrA he too, she too; him too, her too [third person singular additive focal pronoun]

wīstawāw PrA they too [third person plural additive focal pronoun]

wītha PrA he, she; him, her; his, hers [third person singular personal pronoun]

wīthawāw PrA they, them, theirs [third person plural personal pronoun]

Other books in the First Nations Language Readers series:

wawiyatācimowinisa /
ᐊᐧᐃᐧᔭᑖᒋᒧᐃᐧᓂᓴ /
Funny Little Stories
narrated by Cree-speaking students,
instructors, and Elders;
edited by Arok Wolvengrey

Nēnapohš āhtahsōkēwinan/
ᓀᓇᐳᐦᔥ ᐋᐦᑕᐦᓲᑫᐃᐧᓇᓐ/
Nēnapohš Legends
narrated by Saulteaux Elders;
transcribed, translated and edited
by Margaret Cote

Ákaitsinikssiistsi /
Blackfoot Stories of Old
written, translated, and edited by
Ikkináínihki *Lena Heavy Shields Russell*
and Piitáákii *Inge Genee*